I0150881

Seoul-Full Letters

Seoul-Full Letters

Mack H. Webb, Jr.
and Celia Webb

Pilinut Press, Inc.

Seoul-Full Letters

Copyright 2008, Mack H. Webb, Jr. and Celia Webb

All rights reserved.
No part of this book may be reproduced, stored in a retrieval system or transmitted by any means, electronic, mechanical, photocopying, recording, or otherwise, without written permission from the author.

Book and cover design by Celia Webb
Cover Photograph by Celia Webb

Pilinut Press, Inc.
www.pilinutpress.com

The Pilinut is the edible seed of the *Canarium ovatum* tree which is native to Southeast Asia. Tasting like sweet almonds, it is eaten for its health benefits including prevention of anemia and for nourishment of the brain and nervous system.

Library of Congress Control Number: 2008933121
Printed in Warrenton, Virginia

ISBN 978-0-9779576-6-8

TABLE OF CONTENTS:

Dedication

To service members, civilians, and their families who embrace the adventures of their overseas assignments

Korean Proverb

Cast no dirt into the well that gives you water.
Don't bite the hand that feeds you.
Don't spit into the wind.

Introduction

In January of 2000, my wife, Celia, visited her assignment officer at the Army Personnel Command. Celia presented her with a 'Dream Sheet'. A dream sheet is a form, which allows service members to list three of their most desired places for their next duty station. Celia's list included............Dream on! The assignment officer listened politely, typed a few keystrokes on her computer, printed out a page, and handed the paper to Celia. The paper listed three possible locations for Celia's next assignment. Funny how all the locations were South Korea!

Celia had been stationed there on a one year hardship tour (meaning no -- me!! I was stationed in Texas at the time.) from November 1985 to November 1986. We stayed in close touch during this time period; however, letters and phone calls can not convey everything about a foreign country and its way of life. We didn't want to go through another separation, so Celia took the one job that allowed me to accompany her.

When you live in a foreign country, all the new experiences and people may overwhelm you. Everything is either really bad because you keep comparing it to home (who can top Mom's apple pie?), or everything is really wonderful and you wonder why the U.S. can not be more like - _____ - well, you fill in the blank. After about a month or so, the routine of everyday life kicks in and you start to settle into a new way of life. If you are on a military base, this does not have to be too far off the American practice, but you will still notice some nuances.

1

For instance, most of the civilian personnel working on the U.S. military posts in Korea are host nation nationals (Koreans). This became really obvious on September 12th, 2001, when the army posts were locked down due to the heightened state of alert and most services came to a halt because the Korean civilians were not allowed on the posts. Traffic in Seoul that morning and actually for a week afterward was even more "snarly" than normal as most Korean traffic was turned away at the gates and any American cars were essentially strip-searched before being allowed on any post. Many Korean businesses, which catered to the American community, went bankrupt as a direct result of September 11th. The South Korean nation rallied beside the U.S. during the immediate aftermath and, to date, are the staunch allies they have been for over 50 years.

When I heard we were headed to Seoul, Korea for a two-year stint, I was excited. I had never been to the Orient during my military career. My assignments had been in Europe and the U.S. I wanted to experience for myself life in the 'Land of the Morning Calm'. Little did I know I was about to have some of the most interesting experiences of my life.

Korea is a captivating country with a 5,000-year history. Koreans are very proud of their homeland and are eager to show foreigners what Korea has to offer. Some of our best experiences occurred when we got off Yongsan Garrison, and explored the city of Seoul or the countryside.

The normal progression of someone's going to live for a few years in a country other than his own, is at first excitement about a new adventure, then a sense of belonging, and finally a new excitement as the assignment is ending and a new one looms. The letters in this book detail our adventures, encounters, and experiences of everyday life in South Korea. Oh yes, names have been changed -- so no worries.

Korean Proverb

A turtle travels only when it sticks its neck out.
If you don't buy a ticket, you can't win the raffle.

Korean Cultural Tip

Confucian[1] ethics remain the basis of Korean society. So here is a quick review of the order of importance assigned to different relationships.

1. The king is the mainstay of the state.
2. The father is the mainstay of the family.
3. The husband is the mainstay of the wife.

Also, Confucian ethics provide an outline for the attitudes one must have in certain relationships.

1. Between friends, trust
2. Between elder and younger, respect
3. Between husband and wife, distinction in position
4. Between father and son, intimacy
5. Between king and ministers, loyalty

Korean Proverb

No time to open the eyes or the nose.
Too much to do, so little time.

Hello, from the Land of the Morning Calm!   29 Sep 00

> In Korea sweat pours down my neck
> At home clean and pressed now a wreck
>> I feel kind of quirky
>> Like a self-basting turkey
> Korea is as hot as...well...heck

Korea greeted us with steamy, torrid conditions. So it has been to date. We walk into the house from outside, feeling akin to steamed lobsters! I guess in my case it would be steamed mussels (pun intended).

Fruits and vegetables, if left on the kitchen counter for two days, will be fungus-covered. They are rotten on day three. Good gosh, I can only imagine the weather conditions that my father and other soldiers had to endure in Vietnam. It's no wonder jungle rot and trench foot were so prevalent.

Seoul has been besieged by rain showers. Of course, this is the monsoon season and it's one which isn't getting nearly as many inches as previous years. The problem is that the few inches of rain received comes in a deluge. Before one deluge can drain away, another comes. A number of places on post had to be sandbagged. The rice farmers are in tears. It's time to harvest, but the heads of rice are too wet. I'll bet we will see an increase in the price paid for rice.

On another agricultural note, the Koreans do not use pesticides on their food crops. I'm not sure if they use chemical fertilizers. (*Note, I later learned that they do indeed use chemical pesticides and fertilizers on food crops.) Fruit-tree farmers hang traps in the trees. They also painstakingly wrap every piece of fruit hanging on each tree, in paper. This does a great job of keeping insects and some diseases from damaging the fruit. Talk about labor intensive! I've seen this done with apples, peaches, and grapes. The fruit sold in the commissary is delicious and virtually blemish free.

Celia is doing fine. A few days after our arrival, she contracted a cold. Can you believe it? In this heat?? Oh well, it lasted for about two weeks. The first week she was laid low, the second week consisted of hacks and wheezes. I don't know which was worse. I did not get ill, so was able to take care of her and keep her spirits up. Now she's back to normal, and as strong as an ox (and I'm pleased to convey, not looking like one).

The group of people that she works with are a very nice bunch. We've met several times now on eating outings. Eating and drinking clubs form quickly here. We have been inducted into the Eating Club comprised of members from Celia's unit (the place where she works). The only rule is that one gorges one's self to the max at each outing. No problems so far. Some of the members look as though they are exceeding the max. We'll have to be careful that we don't follow suit. This means more time in the gym.

Who could ask for a better location for housing? Less than a five minute walk to the gym! I could get used to this. The gym is called Collier Field House.

Have a wonderful day!!!!!   (Celia is in Japan this week, so she can't sign.)

Korean Proverb

Even Diamond Mountain should be seen after eating.
Eat first, anything else comes later.

Greetings All,   10 Oct 00

> On a plane to somewhere I once flew
> I looked and saw someone I knew
> A reunion occurred
> On that big iron bird
> All at once there it was - déjà vu

This place is just a haven for seeing people known from other duty stations. Case in point, (**flash back**) on the flight to Korea from Washington State I see a person from my unit in Augsburg, Germany. In 1986 Monica was an always smiling, single Second Lieutenant. Now she is an almost never smiling, married with four very young children, Major. Formerly she was an MI (Military Intelligence) officer. Now she is a pediatrician at the hospital on this post. She also interacts with special needs children. Celia remembers her too, and a date is set to go out to a place called the Seoul Tower for lunch. Monica says she'll pick us up at our house. Okay.

She arrives and it is raining rhinos and elephants. Monica says, "I know it's raining pretty hard, but the girls still want to go." (Oh yes, all four children are girls). Fine with us. If nothing else, we can talk about old times and bring all up to date. Right.

We are leaving post and Monica informs us that she hasn't a clue as to how to reach the tower. The tower is situated such that it can be seen from practically anywhere in Seoul. This means absolutely nothing. Every street we can turn on seems to take us further from the tower. Finally, Celia asks if Monica has a map. Monica hands her an ancient Korean map that is in its final stage before leaving the tatters category. Celia looks dubiously at the disintegrating chart, but manages to make heads and tails of it. She's amazing! Meanwhile, the Korean motorists are pressing on their horns. They have zero patience for confused drivers. They seem especially impatient with our driver and her mini-van load of lost Americans.

The little cherubs in the rear of the van bleat constantly that they are freezing; though Celia and Monica are melting under a blast furnace in the front seats. In her attempt to stay in her lane, listen to directions from Celia above the back seat bleating, and control the temperature in the vehicle; Monica 'accidentally' gives the girls a blast of cold air. This causes them to shriek with gusto. Ha! The scenario continues until we park at the tower's base.

We trundle under umbrellas toward the entrance to the tower, about 150 meters. Young elevator maids welcome us. They wear white satin, campaign-style hats with a royal blue ribbon above the brim, royal blue business suits, with white shirts, and blue ribbon bow ties. White cotton gloves cover their hands. The skirt's length is about four inches above the knees. Nude is the color of their stockings, which end in a pair of royal blue pumps with 2 1/2 inch heels.

The tower from base to tip is 1500 feet. The views from such a height are quite spectacular on clear days. Today, from 300 feet upwards there is heavy cloud cover. So we will gaze wonderingly at the mist. Well, that's not entirely true. We do see snatches of vista. Too, there are placards showing what we might see if we visit again.

Having had our fill of the Vista level, onward to the tower's highest level and a refreshing lunch. Now, I must mention that the area in which we will eat is a huge revolving restaurant.   Only the seating area actually revolves, this will come into play in a moment. On a day like this, it's no surprise that we almost have the place to ourselves. Still, the menus are a looooong time in reaching us. Possessing only 20,000 won, Celia and I opt for the pork cutlet and the Top Dinner (a meat patty of dubious origin and a sausage. Delicious?) The exchange rate at the moment is 1 dollar = 1092 won. 18,000 won is our cost, this includes soups and salads for the both of us. Monica gets the large fruit platter and rice, because her children are finicky eaters. The food is being delivered via snail or terrapin express, which ever is slower. Oh well, it's a good time to relax and converse; or is it?

The children are bored, not a good thing in any situation. One of the girls is exploring the view from the dining room window. A minute later she is squealing, "Mommy, help, I'm stuck!". We look and see the little girl slowly being crushed between the revolving dining portion and the non-revolving tower wall. Most of her left side and part of her head have already been drawn in.

The waiter, hearing screams, runs over to try to move the huge wooden planter behind which the child is being inexorably drawn. It won't budge. Monica, quick in action and wit, pulls her daughter from danger's clutch before it is too late. The waiter is ready to faint as he envisions what the outcome may have been. The child snuffles a bit but recovers quickly. Monica doesn't seem phased at all by the ordeal, so we don't overreact either.

Our food is rocketed to us and a waiter hovers near our table, I presume to prevent further mishaps. Unfortunately, it is only my and Celia's soups and salads that arrive. The food is Western style, which for us is a small disappointment. The children (I presume they had no breakfast), like starving waifs from Oliver Twist, are watching us eat every spoonful of soup and every forkful of salad. Even Monica is watching. She asks me, "What kind of soup is it?" I say, "I think it's cream of potato." She then asks, "What does it taste like?" I say, "Sort of like cream of potato." At last their food arrives. They tear into it much like ravenous lionesses might dine on a downed wildebeest.

By meal's end the area looks like a well-used battlefield. Leavings litter the tablecloth, chairs, and floor generously. It's not customary to leave a tip in Korean restaurants, but Monica says she feels so bad about the mess she's leaving a tip. I think the entire restaurant's staff gathers around to watch us leave. Another notch for Korean and American relations.

What could cap this wonderful outing? The same little girl that almost became a waffle in the restaurant, gets this mysterious pain in her private parts. She sobs, grabs her parts, and screams to her mother that, "it hurts!" Most of the cries are ignored by Monica. Her daughter finally settles down to periodic oooooowwws. This lasts for about half of the trip home. Then, the little angels all fall into a deep slumber; from which they will not awaken until their mother has carried each of them up the flights of stairs to their apartment. Sigh. Monica says we should get together again soon. Celia readily agrees. That was weeks ago. Celia hasn't talked to her since (Monica's job keeps her working hard and late.). I thought the whole outing hilarious, in a strange way. I didn't even mention the "breast feeding at the table" episode. OH, MY GOSH!

'Til next time,

Korean Proverb

An empty push cart makes more noise.
The talkative one doesn't necessarily know much. (The
definition of a "windbag".)

Dear All,   28 Oct 00

Last night we went to see a performance of "Nanta". It is the story of kitchen workers who must prepare a wedding feast within an hour. However, they keep getting distracted by the rhythms they can create with common kitchen items. It is a comedy and absolutely delightful.

Nanta came to our notice when we read about it in the "Seoul Word", an English language newspaper. We reserved tickets through the USO (United Service Organizations). The theater was located near Toksu Palace which is right in the middle of downtown. We took a cab there because we didn't have exact directions. Traffic was thick and slow-moving, but we arrived at the show place just in time. The Nanta theater holds about 200 or 300 people.

The show opened with slides shown on a gauze screen. The funny comments on the slides had us laughing well before the actors took to the stage. Very few words were used throughout show—action, facial expressions, and amazing beats dominated the performance. It was excellent!

After an encore, we rode the subway to Yongsan station and then walked the rest of the way. It was a long walk for Celia in her dress shoes and her feet were quite sore by the time we reached home. But what an enjoyable evening we had!

More later,

Dumpling Soup *(Mandukuk)*

Mandu means dumpling. In this recipe the dumplings are boiled, but can also be served fried. Either way, they taste delicious.

Mandu skins:
3 C flour
2/3 C water
1/4 t salt

Sift flour and salt together twice. Add water to flour mixture a little at a time, mixing until dough is stiff. Wrap the ball of dough in a wet towel and set aside.

Broth:
1/4 lb. beef, finely sliced
8 C water
1/2 T soy sauce
Black pepper and salt to taste

Combine ingredients and boil.

Filling:
1/2 lb. beef, finely ground
1/2 C bean curd, mince
1/2 C mung-bean sprouts, parboiled and chopped
1 C cabbage, chopped
4 mushrooms, parboiled and chopped
1 egg, beaten, fried, and cut into thin strips

Flavoring:
1 T soy sauce
2 t salt
2 T green onion, minced
1 t garlic, minced
1 T sesame oil
Black pepper to taste

Brown the beef in hot oil in a frying pan, and then finely mince or grind the beef. Combine the bean curd, mushrooms, mung-bean sprouts, cabbage, and green onion. Squeeze mixture in a clean towel to wring out moisture.

Shape the dough into a sausage-like roll, cut into slices, and roll each slice to form a thin disk.

Mix the browned meat with the squeezed vegetable-bean curd mixture and combine with flavoring ingredients. Place about 1/2 T dumpling filling on each flour shell.

Seal edges with fingers and shape into half moons or small crown-shaped pieces. Add the dumplings to the boiling beef broth. When they float to the top, add 1/2 C cold water and bring to a boil again. Transfer soup to serving dishes and garnish with thin strips of fried egg.

Korean Proverb

Thunder out of a clear sky.
Trouble.

Dear Sis,   30 Oct 00

We did receive the box you sent, it arrived today. In the last letter I sent you, I said that we were close to everything. Close is relative. We have three post offices here, which is a good thing. While I was at the post office to mail a letter, an evacuation order was given. There had been a bomb threat. Not at the post office, but at a building nearby. The military police were securing several blocks. They are not taking any chances after what happened to the USS Cole. Such is life.

There is another post office close to our house, it's about an 800 meter round trip walk. The post office where we pick up large packages like the one you sent is a two mile round trip walk (no problem). But the unit mail room, where we pick up letters and small packages that were mailed to us, is a four mile round trip trek. And it's uphill both ways! (Only in Korea!) But at least there's no snow... yet. So imagine how happy I am when at the end of my quest to the unit mailroom, I find a letter from you in our box! It is a feeling, I believe, akin to finding at the end of one's quest, the Holy Grail! But I digress...

I was the one who picked up the package. Consequently, Celia doesn't know what you actually shipped. I noticed the heart you drew between the Celia and Mack. Such nice little touches of extra. I opened the box, just in case you included some special instructions. WOW! Celia is surely going to have a happy Christmas, so many presents! All of them so beautifully wrapped. The wrapping paper is a very delightful selection, and the musical notes are a definite 'score' (but it's not a tune I recognize). However, tonight we are going to have a 'popping good time' with all of the bubble wrap that was in the box!

Ooooo! There goes that dog again! We live in a duplex. The neighbor's dog is going nuts right now. They either lock him in the house while they're gone or leash him up outside. If he's inside he whines, squeaks, and barks to get out. If he's outside, he slips out of his leash and roams the neighborhood. He usually ends up asleep on the lawn by our front door.

Did you get lots of Trick or Treaters knocking at your door? We did, probably 150 or so. The interesting thing is that about 70% were full-fledged Koreans from babes in arms to teenagers. They were going around with their American friends. The costumes they wore were quite interesting. I wonder what they are going to do with all the candy they collected, since Korean children don't normally eat such sweet candy.

Sister dear, you are a treasure beyond price or measure! Thank you again,

Korean Cultural Tip

Names are considered special and not to be used casually in Korean society. Far better to address someone by his position, trade, profession, scholastic rank, or an honorific title like "teacher" or "uncle". If you insist on using a name, use the formal "Mr. Kim" or "Miss Han" instead of the first name which would imply an intimate relationship.

Korean Proverb

The other person's rice cake looks bigger.
The grass is always greener on the other side of the fence.

Dear All,   5 Nov 00

The temperatures here are starting to drop. The leaves are turning shades of yellow, orange, and red. However, if people want to see a profusion of fall color, they must travel for four hours, to a place called Mt. Sorak. It's 4 hours east of Seoul and just a stone's throw from the Demilitarized Zone (DMZ)[2].

Speaking of the DMZ, we were there recently. It is one of the places that a visitor to Korea must see, mainly because there is such an aura of mystery surrounding it. Because Celia is the officer in charge of Staff Operations here, we were able to receive the VIP tour. Really what you get is a plush vehicle for touring and a deeper explanation into the military and civilian goings-on at the DMZ.

North Korea has a huge speaker system, 7 stories high, that blasts propaganda towards South Korea 24 hours a day, 7 days a week (even the housing area where we live now, is sometimes littered with communist propaganda!). We did get a chance to step over into North Korea. Basically it's a step in, step out situation and gives no sense of North Korean daily life under its current regime. However, when we gaze across the border into North Korea, I am reminded of when I was in East Berlin in 1985. It seemed like time had stood still there, and that they were still living as they did 40 years ago, although it was not at all war torn, because they had rebuilt their roads, buildings, and monuments (mostly with the aid of Russian funds). North Korea is still bolstering its military. This is in spite of talk of a North and South Korean reconciliation.

And now, Celia has a few words to say...

I've had the opportunity to do a little helicopter flying around Korea, with the purpose of checking equipment installations at several remote sites. The helicopter gets us as close as it can to a site and then we hike the rest of the way. Fortunately, the sites I have visited so far have been fairly close to the landing zone! At the last one I visited, we dug up the equipment and replaced it with a new system. Of course, we had to carry the new one in and the old one out and, wow, were they heavy!

Mack and I are looking forward to a dinner cruise on the Han River which flows through the center of Seoul. It is scheduled for Saturday night. Afterward we will go up Seoul Tower and view the lights of the city.

We have been enjoying reading, doing puzzles, watching videos, and traveling around Korea. It is hard to believe we have already been here three whole months!

Best wishes for a Happy Thanksgiving! Love,

Korean Cultural Tip

Maintaining *kibun* is very important to enjoying a friendly relationship with a traditional Korean. *Kibun* can be roughly translated as "mood" or "face". It is sometimes considered better not to tell the truth if it would hurt someone's *kibun*. Truth is desired if it also brings joy and an increase in self-esteem.

A typical example of how you might experience a Korean's desire to maintain your *kibun* is when he gives a promise to complete a project by a certain date you set, even if he knows there is no way the deadline can be met. He is trying to make you happy. Frustrating to the Westerner, but considered polite, thoughtful, and more gentle by the Easterner.

Korean Proverb

A time when tigers smoked cigarettes.
Used to describe something which is very outdated.

Hey Doc!!!   14 Nov 00

I hope you haven't given up on hearing from me. We have been having no end of trouble with our E-mail account. The military base we are stationed on in Korea, is upgrading the communications and electric systems. They literally had the 4 inch cables ripped out and lying in the street. Why they did it that way, I have no idea. Anyway, we're back on line.

A well-known bird here is the magpie. Like the pigeons in Rome, the magpies have reached nuisance numbers. This is a bird that used to feature prominently in the folk art of Korea. Now they are not well received even as art subjects. They possess an interesting coloration of black, white, and blue feathers, with four very long iridescent tail feathers. Unfortunately (though some may yell, hooray!), something seems to be plaguing them. Most of the magpies that we see are losing their head feathers. It's quite sad to see them slowly being de-feathered. I imagine it's caused by a mite, except when their pate is clean, they die. We've seen several dead ones in the area. I don't think the birds are dying of West Nile, feather fallout not being one of the symptoms.

Yes, we are in Seoul, Korea, and have been since July of this year. It's a two-year tour. It has tight living conditions (about 12 million people are packed into Seoul and its contiguous suburbs). Protests are often held outside the compound's main gate. It's like no place I have ever been, and I've been a lot of places.

Now having said all of that, you probably think we hate it here. Not at all, we manage to have a good time despite the crowds and congestion. Korea is an interesting place whose history goes back thousands of years. Every chance we get, we go out and explore the countryside, try to learn something new about the culture, and learn more of the language. I think Celia and I could be happy any place, as long as we are together. We've been together now for almost 20 years.

Celia was just promoted to Lieutenant Colonel (25 October), and has one more tour of duty before she is eligible to retire from the Army. I suggested she stay in until she no longer likes what she is doing, then we can transition to civilian life and do something totally different.

You know my mother passed on to Glory some years ago. I can't tell you how much I miss her. Sometimes, I just can't believe that she is gone. She was such a wonderful person. She remains in my heart and there are times when I long to hear her voice again. My father had three strokes after my mother passed. I believe it was due to extreme grief and pressure. Mother was the glue that held the family together, she's gone and now it's nothing but chaos.

I've rambled on a lot and should close for now, but I'm glad we've connected again. Please tell your family I said hello.

I hope you have a great day and that your holidays are wonderful.

Korean Cultural Tip

The Korean language has many levels of formality and the endings of words signify the relationship between the people talking. Relative differences in age, gender, social status, and length of acquaintance all make a difference in what endings are used. Learn to use the polite form first!

Korean Proverb

Reading into an ox's ear.
It is futile to try to influence someone too stubborn or stupid
to benefit from your wisdom.
"falling on deaf ears"

Dear All,   16 Dec 00

Kim chi. It's everywhere, it has even been deemed the "Official National Food" here, and is one of the ten symbols chosen to explain the Korean heritage to foreigners. There is always some contest or another to see who in Korea can make the best *kim chi.* There are over 150 different types, of which I've tried about ten, you get used to them after the tongue numbs up a bit.

There are some special ingredients that go into making *kim chi,* and it was once a practice to place it in huge earthenware crocks and bury it (usually in the fall) for about six months. Yummy! That practice has all-but-fallen by the wayside since open land is scarce. Only a few (fortunate?) home owners possess a few square yards of land in which to bury their lead-glazed earthenware *kim chi* pots. Of course, the lead leaches into the *kim chi.* It reminds me of a book I once read about the ancient Romans and their lead-glazed drinking vessels. Not to worry though, *kim chi* made for the masses, is made in stainless steel vats. In any event, the aroma of *kim chi* permeates the body the way garlic does. Dogs here used to bark at us because we smelled of beef, not any more...Come to think of it I haven't seen many large dogs around here lately.

Once and for all, let me say that the rumors are true. Man's best friend is a featured item on the entree menu. Now wait a minute, it isn't as though the cooks grab any mongrel unlucky enough to be passing the restaurant at meal time. Dogs are especially raised for the grill, like one might raise cattle or chickens. We haven't tried this delicacy, so I can not comment on the taste. However, when a Korean says the hot dogs are on the grill you can believe it. (A quick word on meat butchers. Korea is **very** class conscious. There is even a hierarchy when it comes to butchers. At the top is the beef butcher, then the pork butcher, and at the bottom is the dog butcher.)

A part of Celia's duties involves visits to some pretty rugged sites; areas requiring chain saws and machetes to clear paths for walking. She spends a lot of time flying around in Black Hawk helicopters to get close to the sites. Celia enjoys the rides; they don't make her air sick. Along the way, she gets some really great views of Korea from a height of about 2000 feet. Looking down, Celia noticed there are thousands of acres of crops under six-foot high hoops covered with plastic. This is done in an effort to extend the growing season of (what else?) vegetable crops for making *kim chi*! Hooray! The helicopters take her pretty close to the Demilitarized Zone (DMZ).

The DMZ, which has been in existence for more than 47 years, is a strange place to visit. What is it like? The DMZ itself, is beautiful. No humans traverse the actual area. It is full of mature trees, wildlife, and plants and flowers that grow nowhere else in Korea. Basically it's virgin land, at least untouched over the last 47 years, and with good reason. There are about four hundred meters of land mines (on the north and south side) that must be negotiated before you can pick the flowers. Wait! Come back!! I forgot to tell you about the razor wire, the machine gun nests, the Claymore mines, and other hidden traps.

This is serious business! Most of the wildlife left in Korea is in this small area. Isn't that sad? It's because much of the wildlife was killed during or just after the Korean War, when people were so desperate and hungry. The Japanese, who occupied Korea[3] from 1908 to 1945, sent all of the trees that they could to Japan for making houses and such. What was left in Korea had to be used as fuel for heating and cooking what little food the Koreans could find. The situation in Korea was deplorable. But, South Korea has, for the last ten years, undertaken a reforestation program that is being very successful.

We have learned so much, but there is still so much to learn, including the Korean language. We are finding it very difficult to learn Korean or *Hangungmal*[4] as it is properly called. It's easy to learn to say the words, but using the right meaning at the right time is a problem. (Example; in *Hangungmal* there are over 20 words for 'wife', depending on whom you are talking to). Normally, we have the bad habit of mixing many of the languages we know into one sentence. It's wise never to use Japanese in conjunction with *Hangungmal*, it will get you nothing but scowls. Don't even say 'hi', because it sounds too much like the Japanese word for 'yes'. The Koreans and the Japanese have an ongoing feud somewhat similar to that of the Hatfields and the McCoys.

Combine *Hangungmal* with Chinese.
You can mix it with Greek all you please.
Spice it up with some Russian,
Or throw in some Prussian.
But don't mix *Hangungmal* with Japanese!

My one run-in with using Japanese was during a USO tour to a village. After a long bus ride, on which I ingested plenty of fluids, the first thing I looked for upon arrival to the village was a latrine! I asked a man who was sweeping the sidewalk, where the restroom was and he pointed the way. In Korea, women clean both male and female latrines, during business hours. It is not unusual to see males corralled at the urinals, trying to find some privacy; while the cleaning lady mops around and between their feet! When I entered and saw what was happening, I decided to use one of the toilet stalls instead. I know the cleaning lady saw me go into the stall, she looked me right in the eyes. However, as soon as I shot the flimsy stall door lock, she started rattling the door. "In a minute", I said. She started rattling with more force. I thought, "Ooh man!", remembering a Jekyll and Hyde movie I once saw. Then I said, "No *Mamasan!*", as I tried to hurry. (I thought *Mamasan* was the Japanese word for Miss. I found out later that *Mamasan* is actually a Japanese reference to a working woman …albeit one who works in the sex industry. Oops! I will not be using that word again! I should have said *Agima*, the Korean word for Miss). It was not the magic phrase. She banged the door, the door lock surrendered, and the door flew open. *Ma...uh...Agima*, almost bowled into me! I was finished by this time. She looked at me, her jaw a little slack. She shuddered slightly as if coming out of a trance, turned on her heels and walked away; the mop in her hand leaving a trail of dirty water. Outside, the man with the broom said in English, "It is very embarrassing to have women in men's toilet." I said, "It sure is!" Was it the Japanese or the Jekyll juice that set her off? We may never knooow...

I've been asked to be one of Santa's elves. Last year Santa was attacked by some teenagers. They were pulling his beard and snatching at pieces of his clothing (their stockings should have been filled with barnyard leavings!). So I am to be elf/Santa guard. The elf costume can be rented from the recreation center on main post. Celia and I thought that I should go right away and reserve a costume before they run out of my size. Okay.

I rushed over to the Recreation center, where behind the counter were two elderly Korean gentlemen. "May I help you, sir?", one asked. "Yes, please", I said. "I would like to check out one of your elf costumes". "Okay sir, who is it for a man or lady?" "Me." I said. His eyes got wide. "You?!" Now I have to tell you that the average height of a Korean male is 5'5" and very slim, so I hardly classified in his mind (I imagine) as an elf. "Oooo", he said, "I don't know if you will fit." He retrieved the largest costume, and I contorted into it.

There, it fit perfectly. The costume consisted of a green suede pull-over shift-like shirt, similar to the one Peter Pan wore, a matching belt and cap. I decided it would work okay for one night if I didn't breath too deeply. The trouble came when I tried to get it off, which I found I couldn't do by myself. I asked the man behind the counter for assistance. I bent over, he pulled, and I went into my "snake shedding his skin" routine. It wasn't long before the shirt started to rip. The man said "Uooo, uooo!", each time he heard a rip.

Finally after about five minutes and some fancy muscle manipulation, the shirt was off (and we dispersed the crowd that had gathered to watch the spectacle, **me**). The man looked at the shirt, then at me, and said, "Ah chi chi chi chi chi", which translates to "What the heck were you thinking?!" (The shirt, for all of the ripping sounds, didn't readily reveal any signs of damage). Well, after that episode, Santa figures I should be a reindeer instead. Great idea, a few choice branches glued to a headband and voilà, Rudolph the weightlifting reindeer!

Hope your holidays are happy!!!

Korean Cultural Tip

Laying your chopsticks on the table indicates you are finished eating. If you are still hungry, lay your chopsticks on the edge of your bowl.

Always leave a little something on your plate to indicate you had plenty to eat and are satisfied. Licking your plate clean says that your host didn't feed you enough which would be a major embarrassment for him.

Graciously pour tea for others at your table but never pour for yourself.

Talking while eating interferes with the proper enjoyment of the meal and isn't done. Plenty of opportunity for conversation, entertainment, and singing comes after the food has been consumed. In fact, you can expect to be called upon to provide some entertainment for the group, so practice your singing and poetry recitation. A favorite is John Denver's "Country Roads". You don't have to be good, just willing.

Chinese Cabbage *Kim chi* (*Paech'u Kim chi*)

Kim chi is the national dish of Korea. While there are lots of cultures that make pickled vegetables, Koreans are the only ones I know of that make such a hot version. Additionally, traditional recipes of winter *kim chi* included salted anchovies and/or shrimp. *Kim chi* promotes health in a number of ways. During the winter when both vegetables and fruits were normally not available, *kim chi* provided vitamin C and prevented diseases of deficiency.

2 Chinese Cabbages
1 ¼ c salt
1 medium white radish
½ c red pepper powder
2 t fresh ginger, finely chopped
1 head garlic, finely chopped
¼ c small green onion threads or chives , cut in 1" lengths
Red pepper threads

1. Cut each cabbage in half lengthwise.
2. Make a brine with 10 C water and 1 C salt and soak the cabbage sections in the brine overnight.
3. When the cabbage has wilted, rinse thoroughly in cold water and drain.
4. Cut one third of the radish into thin strips.
5. Mix the red pepper powder well with water to make a slurry. Add the mixture to the radish strips and mix well until the reddish color is set. Then add the remaining ingredients. Season with salt.
6. Pack the seasoned mixture between each leaf of the wilted

cabbage. Cut the remaining radish into large pieces and mix it with the seasoned mixture.

7. Place the stuffed cabbages and radish pieces in a large crock and put on the lid.

8. Bury ¾ of the crock in the ground and cover the top portion with straw. Or place in a cool storage area where the temperature stays about 40 degrees. Give the mixture three or four days to allow the flavors to blend and then eat as a side dish with a meal. Like other forms of brined and pickled foods, *kim chi* keeps for a long time. In Korea, there are refrigerators built specifically for *kim chi* storage.

Korean Proverb

Can there be smoke from a fireless chimney?
Where there's smoke, there's fire.

Dear All,   18 Feb 01

Korea is a cacophony of smells. Whenever we are outside, we are forced to hack (and wheeze) our way through the thick odor of engine exhaust. Thirty million vehicles help to produce a yellowish-gray haze which hangs in the Korean air, often obscuring nearby mountains from view. Now that Old Man Winter is nipping at our rumps, wood smoke from the fireplaces and the smell of heating oil can be added to the "aroma cornucopia". In the city, the perfume of the sewer is quite prevalent. One reason may be because floor drains in Korean plumbing systems don't have "gas catchers". Normally there is a "U" in the drain pipes, like the one under your kitchen sink. Without this simple addition, gases escape with glee and abandon. Another contributor to the fetid air here, is an open sewer that runs through main post!

A canal on main post is quite wretched,
        Full of something and someone will catch it.
Hey, is that a huge rat?! Oh, a rag,
        But the sight of it's making me gag.
I tell you the whole scene is loathsome,
        Full of tissue and various flotsam.
On really hot days a stench will arise,
        Strong enough to make you cross your eyes.
Originating from a section I'm told,
        Somewhere in the center of Seoul.
Korea has come far, but has far to go,
        Slowly but surely through ebb and through flow.

43

Jokingly, I suggested to Celia that we get a canoe and paddle down the canal. Well, if we close our eyes really tightly (to keep them from watering) we could imagine we are paddling a gondola in the waters of Venice. We could float lazily along the burbling water. Celia was not amused. I wonder, was it a trick of the light, or did she really turn a light shade of green?

With the New Year come new resolutions. A Korean gentleman who works in the post library, has vowed to stop drinking and join a gym. This is no mean feat! He offered to take me to lunch at a Korean restaurant, if I would show him the proper weightlifting and exercise techniques. He pays 60,000 Won a month for his membership, about 50 dollars U.S. That's a lot of money here. The gym is more like a discothèque, with its red, yellow, and green lights in the ceiling, and party music blasting. I was delighted to find the gym was sparkling clean. Not like the gyms on post, which haven't been dusted since General McArthur landed on the South Korean shore!

After spending about 40 minutes at the gym, we went to lunch. During the course of the conversation, he asked me how I liked Korean food. "Oh!", I said, "I like it a lot!" He asked what some of my favorites were. Well, here was a chance for me to show him that I knew the Korean names for the dishes (instead of saying, "I like that dish with all of the tentacles in it.").

So I started..."*Bulgogi* (grilled beef), *Kalbi tang* (short rib soup), *Kogi* (fish), *Chopchee*"...Here, he lifts his eye brows and gives me a strange look. *"Chopchee?"* he asked. "Oh yes!" I exclaimed, *"Chopchee* is one of my favorite foods. In a book at the library, I found a recipe for it. I've even made it at home." He was silent, his brow knit in thought. I could sense that he wanted to tell me something but wasn't quite sure how. Then he said in a shy voice, "Hmmm, maybe you mean *Chopchae?"* "What's the difference?", I asked. "Well", he said looking a little embarrassed, "you just said that you like to make and eat magazines." After the split second it took for me to take that in, I burst into laughter! A moment later he joined in. We couldn't stop! The other patrons probably thought we were drunk.

The following Monday, Celia and I attended our first Korean language class. Now with a bit of Korean, and a generous helping of Marcel Marceau (the greatest mime ever), we get our points across. (No more National Geographics and soy sauce for me!)

Over the holiday season, we visited a Korean orphanage. Twenty five soldiers and family members from Celia's unit piled into two large vans. We took with us over $500 worth of pizza and 73 presents, one for every child. Never before had this happened at this orphanage.

Our driver, Mr. Lee, is the best driver I have ever seen! Korean main roads are narrow, and the side streets look as though they were only meant for Lilliputians on their bicycles! It was on such a side street that we had to thread our huge American-made "conversion" van. To make things more difficult, the road was meant for two-way traffic to include pedestrians! There were also food stalls jutting into the road from both sides. (I'm not making this up for the sake of drama.) When we saw this, the group of us groaned collectively. The van couldn't back out or turn around. Surely it couldn't get through?! I thought about the action movies I had seen, where the vehicles plowed through fruit and vegetable stalls (I've seen a lot of movies!). I was hoping we could avoid that kind of action. Pedestrians tried to become as one with the walls and stalls, to allow us to pass. Others took to their heels, and shuffled back the other direction, preferring not to risk getting their feet run over.

Traveling at the speed of one mile a day, we inched past vendors and oncoming vehicles with only millimeters to spare. What a sight! Shopkeepers bolted from their shops to watch, ready to give us a bill for any produce we might have bruised. Some took a more active role and guided us past obstacles (their fruit). Needless to say, we were extremely late. The director of the orphanage ran down the road and helped guide us. We had stayed in contact with him via cell phones. We finally reached the orphanage. Bleary-eyed children greeted us with cheers and songs! After about an hour of songs and skits (it was obvious the children had practiced really hard on them), we moved to the dining hall to eat.

That night was the only time I have witnessed a child (a little boy of about four) eating a cupcake with chopsticks. I didn't think it strange, I eat cheese curls and potato chips with a fork. This child and I became fast friends. He lounged on my knee as he contentedly ate his meal. Celia imagines he was happy to have an older male around.

At meal's end, it was time to receive and open gifts. Gifts ranged from long underwear to radio-controlled cars. The children were delighted, and the joy and excitement glowed on their faces. I'm glad we had the opportunity to participate in such a happy event.

Post script: Santa's elves...Celia and I helped Santa and his wife present presents to children and adults. We went as elves, dressed in red and white Santa hats (in lieu of antlers). Traffic was horrendous! We got way behind schedule (that's right, the children were bleary eyed). Our delivery list took us all over Seoul. If a parent or spouse wanted gifts delivered, he could give them to Santa beforehand, or leave the gifts outside the front door, or when Santa rang the doorbell covertly give the gift to Santa then. An almost equal number of all three methods were used. I found it interesting that all of the children at or under the age of four were terrified of Santa. I do not know if it was the suit, the beard, or both. They would take one look at Santa and run away as fast as their little legs would carry them. No amount of coaxing from parents could get them onto Santa's knee. If they were babes in arms, they pressed their faces to their mothers' shoulders and WAILED!

The older children were happy to receive a visit from Santa. Teenagers were torn between being glad to get the visit and being afraid that their friends might find out. Santa was in good spirits until we reached a military housing area called Hannan Village. Hannan Village is 15 story high-rise living at its worst. Teenagers and younger children like to hang out in groups in the building's shadows. You get the idea...

It was dark by the time we reached the village. As we neared the first high-rise, Santa began to visibly perspire. "This looks like the spot where I was attacked last year!", he said. There was a gang of teenagers blocking the sidewalk ahead of us. "This is it!", he said in a raspy whisper, "This is the exact spot!" I began to wonder if more had happened last year than I was told about. He dropped back a little, I stayed ahead of him. If Celia and Santa's wife were worried, it didn't show. We passed the teens and with trembling hands, Santa quelled them with peppermint candy canes. In the end, the only trouble we received was from two children who were both about seven. The little rapscallions threatened to kill Santa if he didn't deliver to each of them, a Nintendo Game Boy. I closed the door in the little rapacious faces. Sad is the time when Santa is receiving death threats from children.

Korean Cultural Tip

The use of the word "yes" often only means "I heard you" and should not be taken as agreement. Koreans view this as a way of saving your face by not disturbing your *kibun*. They will try very hard to avoid saying "no" as this causes the other person to lose face.

Disagreement can most often be discerned by their habit of sucking their teeth when they disagree. The louder the sucking sound, the more strongly they disagree.

Korean Proverb

Rice cakes in a picture.
To long for the unobtainable.

Dear All,   18 Apr 01

Ni hau! (hello in Chinese). Sunny, a classmate of mine when I attended the University of Arizona in the early 90's, lives in Taiwan. Over the years we've stayed in touch through letters and e-mails. As luck would have it, we are now very close to Taiwan. So, last month we went to China. No, we didn't take a slow boat, we took a fast 737.

Gone are the days when a job as an airline stewardess or steward, was likened unto the coveted life of a fashion model. Globe trotting, wearing designer suits, and living a glamorous life were yesterday's appeals. Glamorous? I don't think so. Stewardesses no longer girdle themselves up or torture their toes in stiletto pumps. Also, they don't seem too confident that a flight will reach its destination without a hitch. This became apparent to me as we strapped ourselves in for our flight to Taiwan.

We were fortunate enough to have seats by the emergency exit—extra leg room. Right across from us, and facing us, a stewardess readied herself for takeoff. As the turbo engines throttled up, the stewardess did the sign of the cross. I thought, "Joy! That's the way to relax the passengers!" Then I glanced to my right at the other stewardess, she had clasped her hands and was weeping! Great! At that point the slow boat to China held a very great appeal. However, as you are reading this, it is evident that all went well.

I feel compelled to say something about the quality and selection of the food we received on the plane. Airline food has certainly evolved into something delicious. You'll have to come and visit us, so you can see what I mean! The jokes about the minuscule packets of peanuts which require a photon laser to get them open, are going to have to stop circulating. We weren't even offered peanuts. We had a meal of chicken and pasta with wild mushrooms and green onions. A roll with butter, vegetables, orange juice, a fruit cup, and cake for dessert completed the repast. Celia thinks the military can learn a lot from the airline industry concerning meal ingredients and presentation. Not that the military didn't have a great field rations selection when I was in. I had a choice of gourmet meals. I could either have the dehydrated mystery meat surprise or the desiccated "what's that?" It has been said that the Army moves on its stomach. I think a better saying is, the Army writhes on its stomach after consuming field rations!

We finally landed in Kaohsiung, Taiwan. Kaohsiung is off the beaten path for most tourists. We were the only non-Asians in the airport, so Sunny had no trouble spotting us, as Celia and I were wearing matching jackets. (Ha - got you, didn't I?) In the airports of Germany, there are guards armed with machine guns patrolling the terminals. In Korea, the police patrol the airport with pistols at the ready. At the Taiwan airport, we noticed no such patrols. I found this curious, so I asked Sunny about the crime rate in Taiwan. I was assured that it was a very safe place to live. A day later, we went to a local supermarket to pick up a few items. Celia and I were amazed by the huge selection of exotic fruits, vegetables, cereals,...stun guns and other attacker-subduing gadgets that were for sale. Never before have I seen a place where you buy eggs, bread, a gallon of soymilk, and a stun gun all at the same time. Later, we attended an auction where some of the items that were being auctioned off were stun guns! No one was particularly interested in purchasing one until the auctioneer accidentally shocked himself. After that, they sold like hotcakes! A few minutes later the sound of a stun gun's "sizzle" rushed to our ears, from somewhere outside. No wonder there were no police at the airport, everyone must have his own defense system in his pocket or purse!

From the time we landed, our money was no good in Taiwan. Not just because we only had American dollars and Korean *won*, but because our hosts wouldn't let us pay for anything.

A few blocks from the airport, we stopped at a roadside vendor. Hot meat pies for all. Then a few blocks further we stopped for *Bo-pa*. It's a drink made of fresh milk, green tea, sugar, dark glutinous rice balls (or tapioca) about the size of large pearls, and ice. It may sound disgusting, but it's good tasting. Honest! We drank it through a half-inch diameter straw. This allowed the rice pearls to be drawn up with the liquid. A chilly, chewy treat! Those two stops in such rapid succession set the trend for our stay, as we ate almost constantly.

We said we wanted to experience the real Taiwan, so most of our meals came from street vendors. Some food stalls gave us a basket to fill with tofu, vegetables, meats, noodles, and mushrooms. Our selections were quickly cooked on a stove at street side and served to us as a soup at our table. Delicious! I was a little worried about getting what I'll call 'Kaohsiung's Comeuppance', a form of 'Montezuma's Revenge'. We drank the water, ate the ice, and partook in other culinary "daring do's" without ill effect.

Sue, Sunny's 4 year old daughter, is a true champion when it comes to eating. My goodness! A little bottomless pit. I dared not try to keep up with her. Sue kept saying if I didn't eat I was going to get *shol* (thin). I wasn't worried about that. During the car ride Sue became fast friends with Celia and me. Sunny was surprised that Sue took to us so quickly. It became such that Sue wasn't happy unless she was seated next to one of us. We played games with her, sang songs, and danced. Sue cried when we had to leave. We'll miss her, too.

We stayed at Sunny's parents' house. Choosing from 5 bedrooms, we chose one on the fourth floor. There was a latrine on every floor. The latrines (as in many Asian homes) doubled as shower rooms. I mean the whole room was the shower. The showerhead's water line (4 feet long, for those hard to reach places) is attached to the sink spigots. The tiled floor slopes to a floor drain. The bathroom door doesn't rot as it's made of fiberglass.

Sunny anticipated our every need. Her mother doted on us, she even brought us tea and tangerines in case we got hungry during the night. In the morning we awoke to soft Chinese music playing on the second floor stereo. A faint smell of incense burning somewhere in the house, found its way to our room. Not the over-powering type of the 60's, but one of coconut and herbs. A breakfast of gigantic spring rolls and Earl Gray tea, fueled us for the day's activities.

Once on the road, almost immediately, we stopped at a 7-Eleven for something to eat. 7-Elevens are on just about every street corner. They have food buffets inside, containing all manner of Chinese delicacies at reasonable prices. A few miles down the road, we stopped for a big 15 pound bag of red sugar cane. It was already peeled. Red sugar cane is much sweeter and juicier than the white variety. It was all we could do to keep the juice from running all over creation! Then Sunny passed us a bag of bell fruit. Bell fruit is delightful. As its name implies it's shaped like a bell (or a pear), its skin is maroon and waxy-looking, its flesh is crisp and mildly sweet.

Kaohsiung is an agricultural area, farming fish as well as growing mostly unusual crops. One really popular crop grown there is beetle nut. Beetle nut, when chewed, helps keep the chewer alert. Hence, it's a truck driver's staple. One cosmetic side effect is that it turns the teeth a dull red. Beetle nut can be purchased all along the roadsides, from young, scantily clad women who sit in clear glass huts (think greenhouses). No joke! Apparently business is booming.

We went into several gift and souvenir shops, where Celia talked herself out of buying anything. Even so, everyone we came in contact with was amazingly friendly (keep in mind, this is not mainland China). Always a grin and a hello (in English). Many Taiwanese have taken English language courses, but have little use for English outside the classroom. They were happy that we were willing to converse with them.

Case in point, we wanted to visit the Ken Ting Forest Recreational area, it was closing in 15 minutes (the tour is 2 1/2 hours). A man who was volunteering there as a guide, nabbed us and took us in anyway. He was more excited than we were. It was a chance for him to practice his English. He spoke good English, though he denied it profusely. At the time, it was so windy that we had to shout to hear each other. This happened at every park, not the wind and shouting, but the elation the guides showed when they found that we spoke English. After our tour, we went to the beach to watch the sun set over mainland China.

At the time, China was experiencing a colossal, annual sand storm. This storm was so big and dense, that it totally blocked out the sun before it had set! That sand storm has hit Korea and sand is every where. The Koreans call this sand storm, *Hwangsa*, which means yellow sand, (hmmm). How does one cope with it? Stay indoors.

We visited the 'eternal fire'. We went at night so as to get the best effect. The eternal fire is a huge ring of fire in the middle of a grassy field. All over Taiwan there are underground gas pockets. Slowly, they work their way to the surface and are set aflame. It has been happening for many years. The eternal fire was diminishing, but since a recent earthquake it has become brighter. Police patrol the area frequently, to stop people from cooking meals over the flames. Someone had left in haste, leaving a metal grill propped over the blaze.

Another place we went was the "Taiwan Aboriginal Cultural Park".

> At the Chinese folk village you pay a small fee
> Then have all the day to see all you can see
> > Entertainment was waning
> > Till I got a caning
> Then the whole place was filled with much glee

Yes, I was caned. To think I would travel half-way around the world and was beaten with a bamboo cane is absurd. It was like this...we were at the Cultural park. Someone suggested we wander into the building where the Aborigines were engaged in their traditional songs, dances, and skits. That sounded interesting. Only a few minutes were left of the show and audience participation was being encouraged. There was a wedding ceremony, and it was suggested that I join in; I declined. Soon, there was another skit and another chance to participate; I declined again. Then, as the final skit was to begin, I was all but hauled to the stage!

Some of the Aborigines spoke surprisingly good English. I was told to grab a 15 foot bamboo spear and go to the center of the stage. There were about 20 other "volunteers" on stage with me. We knelt on one knee, with the spears pointing skyward. On the count of three, we were to try to impale a ball that was tossed into the air. Three tosses yielded three winners who received feathered headdresses, shell necklaces, and high honors. The sorry losers, of which I was one, were required to bend over for a whack from a bamboo cane. First we had to give thanks, in the native tongue, for what we were about to receive!! It was all noise and absolutely no pain involved. (Celia is making me write that part so you won't worry!) The crowd thought it was hilarious, even Celia was laughing! (Ooooo) As an ending, we danced a ceremonial friendship dance, we all sang while holding hands. Celia joined us for that part. In all, a trip we shall never forget!

Have a great day!!

Korean Cultural Tip

When handing an object to a Korean, do so with either both hands or with your right hand extended and your left hand touching your right elbow. This tradition comes from an assassination of one of the Korean emperors who was killed by a person pulling a sword out of his long sleeve. Touching your right elbow indicates you have nothing else up your sleeve.

Korean Proverb

It is dark at the base of the lamp.
Two meanings:
Not being able to see the nose on your face.
Searching for something that was right in front of you the
whole time.

Greetings All!   11 May 01

There is hardly a time when Celia and I can stroll through or sit in a public place without children coming up to us to talk. We don't mind, but at times it can seem a bit overwhelming. It's never just one child; they are too shy for that. They come in groups or droves.

Generally, the first thing the children will do, after they have scrunched together in front of us, is giggle a lot. There seems to always be a natural leader within every group. The boldest, the "joker", or even the smallest of the group, almost always a male, might speak up first. He will say, "Hello, how are you?" (Giggles from the other children). I say, "Hello, I am fine. How are you?" (Lots of laughs and giggles.) The children are pleased with this "text book" response.

Once the ice has been broken, the questions pour in, all at once. "Where are you from? What is your name? Do you like Korea?" I must point out that this last question, "Do you like Korea?", is very important. The correct answer to this question is always, "Yes!" or "I like it very much!!"

In fact we do like Korea very much. You have heard the worn-out travel guide pitch, "There is something for everyone in..." Well, it holds true for Korea. Never mind that everything will have a Far Eastern twist. If you don't find what you are looking for, it is because you have not looked in the right place.

What's that you say? The children? Oh yes, back to the children. The groups of children that encompass us on our outings are not unsupervised. They are usually chaperoned by teachers from the school they attend. It is a regular practice for children to spend a Saturday morning at some cultural site like a museum taking notes and receiving lectures. So seeing us, Americans, is a wonderful distraction.

The chaperoning teachers are okay with their little charges interacting with us and they even encourage it. The English language is a staple in the young Korean student's curriculum. What better way to get hands-on practice than with willing native English speakers?

There are times, however, when the little darlings become rowdy with excitement and sympathetic adults must step in to try to calm them down. One such incident happened at a museum Celia and I were visiting.

Flashback We really enjoy museums. As we stroll through the halls marveling at one exhibit after another, we catch the eye of one of the roving museum guards. He can tell we truly appreciate what the building houses and that we are enjoying ourselves. Smiling, we offer him a slight bow of salutation. He returns our gesture and we continue on our way.

Shortly after this exchange, from the corner of my eye, I notice a little boy pick up our trail. Keeping a respectful distance he begins to follow us. When we stop, he stops. When we move, he moves. At one point I turn to look directly at the child and he quickly turns away. I have been on enough outings to know what is to happen next. The child is relentless. Eventually I catch his eye and smile at him. This causes him to trot off and return moments later with several of his friends in tow.

Now he feels comfortable enough to approach us and say, "Hello". From there it is an avalanche of questions from all directions. More of his mates join in and the encounter becomes quite loud.

The guard, whom we earlier greeted, seeing that we are inundated, rushes over and shoos the children away. I do not understand everything he is saying to them, but it is something to the effect of, "Let them enjoy the exhibits in peace". His work done, the guard gives us an apologetic smile and turns to leave.

No sooner does he turn the corner than the children converge upon us again, asking questions and jockeying for position. The guard, hearing the din, returns to shoo the giggling children. He has to do this two more times before he decides to be our personal guard.

It may seem strange to Westerners, my referring to the guard taking it upon himself to guard us, but South Koreans take it very personally if a foreigner does not have a good experience while in their country. Most natives we meet are committed to showing this country in the best possible light. Because of the guard's vigilance, Celia and I finish our tour of the museum uninterrupted. Before taking our leave, we thank the guard who seems genuinely pleased to have helped us.

We make our exit and are outside for about five minutes before the pack of children from the museum sprint over to us. This time they are brandishing small notebooks and pens or pencils. They want our autographs. I do not quite understand what the children do with the autographs they collect, but almost every child we have encountered during our outings has had an autograph book. It is my guess the books are part of a foreign language class project, whereby the students can show their teachers proof of contact with many foreigners. One can never tell what impact one's behavior will have on another person, especially children who are so impressionable, so we are patient and carefully sign every notebook. After our efforts, we receive waves, giggles, and several handshakes before the children rush to join their beckoning teacher.

Days like this are a large part of what is making our stay in Korea so interesting. Upon our departure from Korea we are sure to take with us many good impressions of this "land of the morning calm". We hope to leave behind many good impressions as well.

Have a wonderful day!

Korean Cultural Tip

It is customary to clap at the end of a meeting.

Korean Proverb

Fixing the stable door after losing the ox.
Closing the stall door after the horse is gone.

Dear All,   5 Sep 01

Most military posts tend to be mini-cities, comprised of everything a soldier or family member could possibly need. This post is no exception. The hospital is just around the corner, the commissary is a ten-minute walk from our house; as are fast-food restaurants and more formal dining places. The library and department store (PX), are a 15-minute walk away. There are four gyms, three furniture stores, a thrift shop, a recreation center, and night clubs. The list goes on and on. There is even a gambling casino, though not a very large one. We don't gamble, but I think it's interesting that the casino is always so people-packed. We know the person who oversees its operation. He said the casino brings in about 14 million dollars a year! WOW!!

This post is divided into two main parts. Each is surrounded by a ten-foot high, two-foot thick, concrete block wall. The wall is topped by strands of barbed wire. One can only enter and exit through a series of heavily guarded gates. Sounds pretty dismal, huh? One gets used to it. At any rate, it keeps the protesters at bay.

There was another protest today at the gate.
Many such incidents happen of late.
A forecasted gathering of a thousand or more,
But the actual number is hardly a score.
I see a man with a bullhorn, his lips flecked with
        foam.
What's that he just yelled? "Yankee, go home!"

Seoul is a city of about 12 million people. In the whole of South Korea, there are only 100,000 Americans. One would think that we are hardly noticeable. However, on any given day, there is a protest just outside the gates of the U.S. military installation in Seoul. The ballyhoo usually concerns the SOFA agreement. No, this isn't an agreement on the part of the U.S. to get a nice, comfy sofa into every Korean household. SOFA means Status Of Forces Agreement. It regulates the jurisdiction and punishment of U.S. soldiers when they have committed crimes in foreign countries (Korea). It sets limits on the amount of land we can occupy and controls the non-taxable items we can bring into Korea. It also regulates how many of the locals we must hire and how much they will be paid.

Anytime a group (usually college students) wants to stage a protest, they must first file for permission at certain offices downtown. So, we have a fair warning of any upcoming protest, days before it actually happens. The police are also alerted. They station themselves between the protesters and the installation's gates. If a big protest is planned, the police will arrive on specially outfitted buses, by the hundreds. Individual buses are modified to serve as latrines, dining facilities, or sleeping quarters. Dressed in full riot gear, the police will sometimes stay for weeks. Such was the case when we first arrived in Seoul. A protest of several thousand was supposed to march to our front gates. Nothing ever happened, and eventually most of the police were driven away on the buses. But at any given time, there is a skeleton crew of police walking patrol just outside the installation's walls. Like mail carriers, they are out during all types of weather. They are at their posts even during typhoons.

You probably did not hear much about the typhoon that blew through our area. We didn't hear much either. It's amazing how little is reported on the Armed Forces Radio and Television Network (AFRTN), concerning the happenings here. In preparation for the typhoon, we stocked extra food rations. Every container in the house, to include sinks and the bath tub, was filled with water. We don't have the large water towers here like the ones in the States. A loss of electricity could have knocked out the water pumps for several days. Luckily the power was out for only 24 hours. The typhoon arrived during the night with wind gusts approaching 130 miles an hour. Trees fell, having been either ripped from the earth or broken off at their trunks. Celia and I could hear them falling on near-by houses! About 100 trees were lost in contrast to the more than 200 ruined last year.

Power lines snapped, and we were plunged into darkness. The wind screamed, carrying with it airborne missiles of every kind. Rain came down in torrents, and its great volume overloaded the post's inadequate drainage system. The surging surplus water, having nowhere else to go, flooded into many low-lying housing units. Valiant efforts were made at sandbagging, but it was useless. Families could only watch in dismay, as their possessions floated around inside their houses. When the morning arrived, we saw that heaps of storm debris littered the streets. The neighborhood was engulfed by that eerie silence that occurs only during power outages. We have been through two typhoons. The second one is hardly worth mentioning. It was bigger (360 miles across), but the part that passed over us did very little damage. I do believe prayer helped. **(All of this during the beginning of September!)** Through it all, Celia and I managed well.

One of the duties of Celia's job is to attend the functions of high-ranking Korean military officials, all in the interest of good foreign relations. This can be very tricky, because Korean officials do not take kindly to women as authority figures.

Recently, Celia and several co-workers went to a restaurant with a Korean General. To say that a lot of drinking happens at such 'get togethers', is an understatement. Everyone in attendance is expected to drink copiously. (Once a female, who attended such an outing, politely declined to drink. The Korean general got upset and said, "By refusing to drink, you not only offend me but my country as well!" He was drunk. But he got his point across, and she drank up.)

At the restaurant, mountains of food of every sort graced the tables. The alcohol flowed freely. There was talk on various issues. The alcohol flowed freely. The food kept arriving in an endless procession. Did I mention that the alcohol flowed freely? It was a mixture of beer and whisky, a concoction called The Bomb. Celia held firm to her non-drinking status, so a designated drinker was selected for her. He had to drink not only his full share, but Celia's share as well. After a while, the inebriated general confronted Celia and asked why she didn't drink. Celia said, "For religious reasons." He sat in thought for a moment, then slowly nodded his head. That was the end of that.

Having gorged themselves to the limit, drinks in hand, they retired to a Karaoke room for some song singing. Karaoke is a favorite entertainment here. Of course, every person in attendance was required to sing a song. In their heavily sauced state, the men couldn't carry a tune. When Celia sang, as so often happens, the men were stunned to silence. Surely it was an angelic voice they heard. They wept salty tears into their drinks. Were they thinking of happy times gone by, of their loving mothers or their childhood? I don't know. She was called back for more solos, new tears flowing at each ballad. Drinking aside, Celia works with good bunch.

Until next time,

Glass Noodles *(Chopchae)*

One of our favorite Korean dishes is *Chopchae*. It is a noodle dish with vegetables and, sometimes, strips of beef.

1 carrot, matchstick cut
1 bunch green onions, chopped
1 bunch fresh spinach, cut leaves in half
10 oz. steak, thinly cut
1 package cellophane or glass noodles, cook per directions, and drain
2 T sesame oil
Soy sauce to taste
1 T sugar
¼ t black pepper
2 T sesame seeds

Sautée steak in sesame oil until browned, add vegetables. Cook until vegetables are translucent. Pour steak and vegetables over noodles. Toss all ingredients until thoroughly mixed. Enjoy!

Korean Cultural Tip

Koreans love to drink alcoholic beverages and want you to enjoy it too. Both official and social functions often involve large amounts of alcohol. It is generally considered an insult not to partake.

There are two marginally acceptable reasons for not participating in the drinking. First is that your health does not allow it and second is that your religious beliefs do not allow it.

As Koreans become more familiar with American ways, there is a degree of tolerance for non-drinkers. However, the bottom line is that non-drinkers will probably be looked at with some suspicion.

Korean Proverb

A small pepper is hot.
Small people can accomplish a lot.

Dear All,   20 Oct 01

I've been in literary limbo lately and I've got a lot of catching up to do. This missive may be taken in small bites and digested slowly.

Celia and I were looking for interesting places in Korea to visit during a three-day weekend. We read about Suanbo, a hot-springs resort not far from Seoul. It sounded interesting so grabbing a map and provisions, we set out on our adventure.

> Suanbo is a hot-springs resort
> It's quite hot I'm here to report
> They use *ondol* for heat
> You are watched while you eat
> And of cash you will leave there quite short

Just outside of post, we hailed a taxi. The driver jammed on the car's brakes to allow us to enter. A motorist behind him missed rear-ending him by an inch. Experience taught us that we should be quick, but before we could finish strapping ourselves in, the cab driver took off like a bat out of...uh...the bat cave (yeah, that's it!). The initial G-force the taxi drivers can create is quite impressive! It wasn't that he thought we were going to miss our bus, it's stock driving behavior in Seoul. Just grip your seat and remember to breathe!

At the bus terminal, we stepped out of the cab and walked on rubbery legs into the station; only to find out that the station we wanted was on the other side of town. Disdaining another ride with the Hyper-drive Cab Company, we took the subway. You can go anywhere in Seoul (one way) on a 50-cent subway ticket. Everyone was very helpful in ensuring that we traveled on the right subway line. We had no trouble finding the proper bus station.

As we boarded the bus, the driver was in the process of warming up the Karaoke system. Every bus here, except city buses, has a Karaoke system installed. Passengers are expected to partake in the singing and even stand up front and sing solos using a microphone. (Groan...) Any time a bus passes, you can hear the boom of the music playing inside. Through the windows you can see people dancing in the aisle. I'm sure that can't be very safe, but there it is. Our driver turned on the TV, selected a Karaoke CD, and CRANKED IT UP REALLY LOUD!! He looked at us and grinned with satisfaction. We were <u>not</u> looking forward to our four-hour bus ride. (That reminds me, I'll have to write you a letter about our trip from Germany to Spain, on the bus from '**The Lower World**'!) Fortunately for us, only seven passengers peopled the bus. So paltry a population didn't warrant the use of the sound system, so we traveled in silence. Celia went to sleep.

Once outside of Seoul, the scenery changes quickly. Tall buildings of concrete, steel, and glass are replaced by one-story houses made of mud and salvaged wood. These are the houses of farmers. Plowed fields surround the houses. I was fortunate to see a rare sight, a person working knee-deep in the mud of a rice paddy. I say rare because in this age, many of the rice farms are mechanized. Four hours later, we climbed into another taxi for the last leg to the resort.

The resort is situated on a mountain top. The engine of the taxi whined and protested as we made our way up the steep, twisting road. The resort was rated as having a 'first class' hotel. Excited? We were. We've since found the Korean rating scheme is different from the one used in the U.S. Hotels here are divided into five groups: super deluxe, deluxe, first class, second class, and third class. There is another class (I'll call it fourth class), it's not talked about much and just the thought of it makes me shudder. You do not want to stay at a fourth-class hotel! As it was, our hotel was akin to a Motel 6. We checked into our room, it was a Western (U.S.) style room. The room faintly resembled the photo in the brochure, taken ten years ago. I did a quick room inspection and flopped onto one of the beds...(Wha-thud!). Mattresses in Korean hotels are firm! How firm are they? Well, consider that the traditional Korean pillow is a block of wood in a cloth sack, albeit a decorative sack.

We awoke in the middle of the night drenched with sweat. The room was so hot, I thought I had missed the first blast from Gabriel's trumpet! Thanks to the Korean heating system known as *ondol*, we were roasting at the resort. Underneath the floors are stone or concrete flues. Traditionally, hot air was vented through the flues to provide heat. Clay or cement would be placed over the stones to protect the residents from noxious gases (sometimes it worked, sometimes it didn't). This type of under-the-floor-heating is called *"ondol"*. Nowadays, hot water is piped through cement floors covered with linoleum. Even so, there is no way to control the temperature from within the room. We were forced to finish the night with the sliding-glass patio door open. The fun never stops!

We had most of our meals at the resort. Since it was the off-season for tourists, we were usually the only two diners in the restaurant. All of the attendants including the cashier, would stand by and stare at us while we ate. Occasionally, they would murmur something to each other while keeping their eyes on us. Their best speaker of English was standing very close, so as to take care of our wants immediately. This establishment was charging almost four times the price of a normal Korean restaurant. I'd be interested to see what they charge during the peak season. The meals are *a la carte*. As we ordered, our waiter became visibly nervous. He kept informing us that each item on the menu was a separate charge. By the time we finished our order (we only ordered four items each), he was glazed with a sheen of perspiration! He knew the food was very expensive. He may have thought because we were foreigners we did not understand the exchange rate, and therefore, would be in the poorhouse after settling the bill. Such was his anxiety, that he did not charge Celia for her small $3.00 cup of coffee, and he gave me a free coffee even though I hadn't ordered one.

While we ate, a robust Buddhist[5] monk entered. He had a cleanly shaved pate, was dressed in the traditional gray cotton uniform with huge prayer beads around his neck, and he carried a six-foot long walking stick. I looked down at his Nike hiking boots, and supposed he was on some pilgrimage of enlightenment. I wondered what his life must be like. Ooh, having to endure the hardships of living a lifestyle in the manner of the ancients. He must, I thought, live at a secluded temple and spend the greater part of his waking hours in meditative reflection. Unbound by the shackles of modern technology, unhampered by... My musings were checked as he pulled out a cell phone and made a call. Oh, well. After finishing our meal and paying some child's way through college, we went on a boat tour.

The president of the tour company, Mr. Yi, sent his personal driver to pick us up at the hotel. Shortly afterwards we were ushered into Mr. Yi's office where we had *"koepi"*[6] (coffee), exchanged business cards, and made small talk. He was surprised by Celia's being in the military and being a lieutenant colonel (LTC). Celia's rank surprises most people, because she looks too young to be an LTC. Women in the Korean military rarely rank above captain. Mr. Yi spoke good English, but soon the conversation dwindled and we sipped our coffee in uncomfortable silence. It must be noted that almost every business transaction (at the better establishments) is preceded by hot coffee. It is considered barbaric to do otherwise. It's no use to try to look as though you are in a rush, just have a seat and start drinking. You will only ever get half a cup, any more is considered impolite. After a few more moments we were driven to the point where we would board the boat. We were well taken care of.

It was a chilly day, but we thought the view would be better if seen from the boat's upper deck. We were right. Mountains towered on either side of the vessel. It was strange and rather sad to think that several fathoms below the boat, there were houses and other buildings that were abandoned when the dam was built. It was lunch time and on the upper deck everyone was gathered into their groups and dishing out food. The Korean community loves to do things in groups.

Having just finished a large meal we weren't wanting anything else to eat. We sat down and within 30 seconds we heard a, "Hello!" I turned around, and returned the greeting to a man sporting a toothy grin. A moment later, the same man was saying, *"Bap, bap"* (*bap* means rice in *Hangungmal or hanguko. Hangungmal* and *hanguko* refer to the spoken Korean language). He was making eating motions with his chopsticks. I tried to convey the fact that we had eaten lunch and didn't think it wise to eat any more so soon. I made chewing motions and patted my stomach. On further reflection, that was not the best way to convey an already full stomach. He probably thought I was trying to say, "Let me at it!" He rushed over and thrust at us a Styrofoam container holding two neatly rolled and sliced *kimbap*s and a pair of chopsticks.

Kimbap consists of rice, carrot, fried egg, cucumber, and other varied ingredients, which are rolled up in dried seaweed sheets and cut crosswise like sushi. They were delicious, Celia ate two pieces, and I rammed down the rest.

We were also treated to some authentic, homemade *kim chi* (W-w-whaaaaa!).

When we had finished, the gentleman took the empty container and threw it away. Then he came back, seated himself beside me, snuggled up, put his arm around me, pulled me close...Ooooh man...and his friend took our picture (whew!). I must have burned a hundred calories during that moment! I never knew older Korean men could be so generous and friendly. We were to be even further enlightened before the boat ride was done...

Having become a couple of "Webbsicles" in the freezing wind on the upper deck, we made our way to the heated space on the lower deck. There was some type of party going on in the cabin area. We sat in the seats furthest from the action, to warm up and listen to the music. All of a sudden this lady is tugging on my arm, and saying something I did not understand. She was smiling and very insistent. Celia said, "She wants you to go up front and dance." She wants WHAT?! I'm sure I told her no at least seven times, but she would have none of it. Well, if I had to go (you know, U.S. relations and all), I wasn't going without Celia. The lady snatched my backpack, (HEY!) unzipped it and started jamming my stuff inside!

Once up front, I felt about as comfortable as I would have on 'the rack'. There were about 60 people dancing and singing in Korean, it seemed like all eyes were boring into me. The room had become extremely warm, and sweat rolled down my back. I faced Celia and swayed to the music like a stalk of wheat on a windless day.

Then that same lady (oooo!) shoved me into the middle of the crowd, someone else shoved a lady in front of me and we were expected to dance together. There was nothing else to do, I started dancing the merengue. The ladies went nuts! Those dance lessons from the Arthur Murray Dance Studio in Severna Park, Maryland have helped me out of a lot of jams! I grabbed Celia and lead her through a merengue and a series of turns, and then we did the conga. While we danced, a line formed comprised of women from age 80 years to 18 months. They wanted to dance with me. Can you believe it?! (This involved touching, which I thought was taboo in Korea unless the couple was married.) The 18-month-old was held in her father's arms, he actually did the dancing for her. (This came as another surprise to me, that he would want her to dance with me. You will notice that I'm surprised by a lot of things over here.) This same man challenged me to a dance contest. Again, thanks to Arthur Murray it was no contest at all.

Meanwhile, Celia, in the midst of a crowd of men and women, was dancing up a storm! She is amazing!! Everyone was laughing and having a good time. I was still perspiring, not from nervousness, but from exertion. When the music finally stopped and the dancing was done, no less than three people offered me their handkerchief to mop my brow. Everyone was shaking Celia's hand. A man whose wife I had danced with, wanted to buy us a drink.

I was unsure what kind of drink he had in mind, I suspected it was one containing alcohol. I tried to convey my dislike for the stuff. I said, "I don't drink." That didn't work. I made the 'Buddha bless you' sign (you know, monks don't drink). That didn't work either, he just kept saying, "Pedo. Pedo, pedo.", and making the 'down-the-hatch' gesture. Finally, because his wife was looking so anxious, I said, "Okay, let's go". On the way to the lounge we passed the captain of the vessel. I had talked with him earlier, and this time tried to get him to interpret for me. He only smiled and patted me on the back. Hmmm. All the while my escort is saying "pedo". In desperation I said, "Pepsi?" He beamed and with energy said, "Pepsi, Pepsi, Pepsi!" I still wasn't convinced, so I said, "Cider?" (Cider is a Korean form of 7-Up) "Aahh, yeh yeh (yes yes) Cider!" So, three ice-cold Ciders were the order of the day.

There were three elderly gentlemen in the lounge; when they saw us come in they beckoned us over. I told them we are '*Meguks*' (Americans), and they all wanted to shake our hands. The eldest of the three held onto my hand, and wringing it affectionately, spoke to me in a sincere, very emotional tone. By the time he let go, he was in tears. As we left the lounge, his friends blew us many kisses. Need I say that I was again surprised? Apparently, during the Korean War they were in Pusan, an area south of Seoul, and are still thankful to the Americans for shielding that area from the North Koreans. I had no vocabulary to say that America was glad to help, so I just said, "*Chun mon nay yo*" (You are welcome.) We had reached our docking point and our drinking companion wanted to walk arm-in-arm with Celia to the dock. Okay, but that was as far as I would go to maintain good foreign relations!

We were met at the dock by the president of the tour firm. (Such treatment!) He had set up a trip for us to visit a Korean folk village. Though we were a little tired and our feet were sore, we knew it would be rude and useless to decline. We were whisked away by his personal driver to the folk village. We've been to three folk villages so far. I'll have to send you a separate letter telling you about those. Otherwise this letter will be **very** long. The Suanbo trip was a great experience for us; another adventure for the book.

Until next time, have a wonderful day!

Korean Cultural Tip

Before any business is discussed, tea or coffee will be offered. The exchange of pleasantries is expected. Only after the refreshment is finished should the conversation progress to business topics. Impatience is a cardinal sin.

Barbecued Beef *(Bulgogi)*

Bulgogi is marinated, barbecued beef. It is delicious. There are also chicken and pork versions. Use the same marinade for any of the meats and grill it up. Originally, *bulgogi* was made with any cut of meat. Now it is almost always steak.

1 lb. round steak, cut into thin strips
¼ C soy sauce
½ C chopped green onions
2 T sesame seed oil
1 T sesame seeds

Combine all ingredients and marinate for at least 1 hour. The best-tasting versions are grilled over charcoal, but you can also pan fry it. Serve with rice, Cos lettuce, and *kim chi.*

Korean Cultural Tip

Relationships are critical in Korean society and protocol is extremely important. Self-effacement in social and business contacts is considered correct behavior, while putting yourself forward is considered brutish and uncultured.

Koreans have a hierarchy of social importance. You will be assigned a spot in the hierarchy too, based on factors such as your age, gender, position title, rank, type of work you do, the fact that you are a foreigner, etc. While most Koreans make a lot of concessions for foreigners and do not expect them to understand the nuances of the hierarchy, it helps tremendously if you treat high-ranking persons or their representatives with a great deal of respect.

Korean Proverb

A frog in a well.
Used to describe someone with no vision or perspective.

Dear All,   6 Nov 01

There is movement in the bushes on our yard, what
can it be?
Say, there it is again, something large by that tree!
I call Celia to the window, and we spy outside a
pheasant.
We smile and surmise the predicament is pleasant.
As we watched through the window feeling pleased,
wouldn't you know;
The fowl did his business right upon our patio.
And as par for the course, mom and "chicklets"
sallied forth;
They dropped their loads at our abode, and with
pluck they headed North.
Pheasants are quite messy birds, and what they do, it
isn't subtle.
Maybe this year instead of turkey, something under
glass I'll shuttle.

Thanksgiving and other holidays are just around the
corner, and that means lots of festivities and eating. Jenny,
my thoughtful sister-in-law, was kind enough to send me a
non-alcoholic fruit cake recipe, and I'm anxious to share it
with everyone!!! To help make your festive eating even
more festive, I'll ship you several fruit cakes. You'll love
'em! They're chock-full of daaates, and nuuuts, and
cherriiies, and all manner of good stuff. Soooo, if I don't
hear from you by November the 9th, I'll suppose you want
at least two and will ship them off.

89

The Koreans observe a Thanksgiving Day too; it is called *Chusok*. It is one of the biggest festivals of the Korean year and it celebrates the bringing in of plentiful harvests before the winter. New clothes are worn and the best of the season's crops such as persimmons, chestnuts, apples, pears, cereals, and wine are placed on ceremonial tables to honor the ancestors. *Chusok* is also a time when city-dwelling Koreans visit and exchange gifts with their kith and kin in the country. South Korea has a population of about 46 million, and about one fourth of that population lives in Seoul. Seoul occupies only 1% of the landmass of South Korea. No wonder Seoul always seems so crowded, because it is! During the holiday, which is actually a four day weekend, Seoul becomes a veritable ghost town. Thirty-one million determined travelers pack the roads and railways of South Korea. Traversing these roads, especially in a taxi, can leave your mouth as dry as gauze and your hair standing on end. And speaking of hair...

One of the first things I was told upon my arrival in Korea, was that all Korean barber shops are off limits to U.S. soldiers and their family members. The reason? I'm told that a soldier entered a barber shop under his own locomotion, but needed a lot of help getting out. He had been paralyzed by the barber! Yowch!! (No, I'm not making this up.) In a Korean barbershop, the price of a haircut includes a head and neck massage. Just sit back while the barber utilizes an ancient Korean massaging technique. Sound relaxing? It was for one soldier. Maybe the barber's attention was elsewhere. He may have been day dreaming about what he was going to do with the big tip the American would give him. Maybe he was remembering that this guy never tipped. I don't know. The end result was a soldier who had to be medically discharged from the military. I cut my own hair and go without the neck massage.

Celia has her hair done on post. She has a really good Korean hairdresser named Ruth. Ruth takes great care of Celia. The prices are easy on the pocketbook too. In the States, a hair cut is $20, here it's $10. A perm State side is $75, here $38. Eye brow waxing $10-vs-$4.50, and they wax the top and bottom of the eye brow. Manicure, $25-vs-$7. Celia's a happy camper!

After Celia returns from the hairdresser, she usually feels like going out to dinner. Once, we ended up at an out-of-the-way Korean restaurant in *Insa-Dong* called *Koong*. It was very informal, as most tend to be, and the food was delicious. The owner of the place is a grandmother of 83. She made *mandu* (filled dumplings) for us from scratch, while we watched. Everything was quite fresh. Green onions, mushrooms, radishes, carrots, greens, *mandu* and a broth comprise the dish called, *Mandu JeonGol* (translation, '*Mandu* Cooked At Your Table").

The meal was put into a stainless steel bowl and, as we looked on with watering mouths, it was cooked at our table on a portable gas burner. Steamed rice and several different *kim chi* side dishes came with the meal. (It may seem that I am always going on about it, but let me give you another quick word on *kim chi*. Whew!! You may know that *kim chi* is vegetable matter such as cucumber, radish,

Chinese cabbage, bean sprouts, etc., that is mixed with fermented anchovies, ginger, garlic, green onion, and tons of red pepper. The mixture is allowed to ferment for a time, which produces a vitamin, mineral, and protein-packed, incendiary creation. After I tried **authentic** Korean *kim chi* for the first time, my tongue felt like it had been dipped in lava! I almost knocked the person next to me over in my pursuit of water. Water was a mistake. With my tongue in so sensitive a state, it was like throwing gasoline on red hot coals. Eating rice has a greater cooling effect, but not much. *Kim chi* will vaporize your taste buds if you're not careful. The mere thought of it is making me sweat!) We finished our meal with soothing cups of chilled tea. Celia had plum tea, and I had citron tea. Both were very enjoyable in taste and aroma.

You too can have a taste of Korea. Here is a recipe for one of Korea's traditional autumn drinks. No need to have firemen standing by for this treat.

Persimmon Punch (*Sujonggwa*)

10 dried persimmons
the weight of the persimmons in fresh ginger roots
6 cups of water
1 cup of sugar
1 T pine nuts
powdered cinnamon

1. Scrape the ginger and slice it thinly. Add the water, and simmer for 1 1/2 hours.
2. Remove the ginger and add the sugar to the liquid, boil for 5 minutes and cool.
3. Carefully remove the seeds from the persimmons and replace them with pine nuts. Add the persimmons to the syrup and allow it to stand for 5 hours.
4. Chill the punch and serve it in a bowl with pine nuts and cinnamon sprinkled on top. Ladle individual servings so that each portion has a persimmon and some stock.

* The quantities may be doubled, or the sugar increased to 1 1/2 cups if a sweeter syrup is desired. Alternatively, the sugar may be replaced with honey. One of the pleasures of this dish is...well, I'll let you be the judge of that. Let me know how you like it.

P.S. You can relax, I was only kidding about sending the fruit cakes. Have wonderful day!!

Korean Proverb

Though you bury a dog's tail for three years, it will not become a weasel's fur.
You can't make a silk purse out of a sow's ear.

Dear All,   2 Dec 01

An-nyeong-ha-se-yo? (Have you had your rice today?) This *Hangungmal* (Korean language) greeting can be spoken any time of the day throughout South Korea.

It was a happy event to have Celia's parents (Mom and Dad) in Korea for two weeks. They came as part of the Korea Reunion Tour, which is offered twice a year. It allows the family of active duty service members stationed in Korea to visit Korea at a discounted price. It also provides them the opportunity to tour some of the fascinating places Korea has to offer.

Mom and Dad landed at the Inchon airport, a new airport that has been open for only a few months. Inchon is a huge upgrade over the old Kempo airport just a few miles down the road from this new airport. The modern design and the vast interior of Inchon are impressive.

Flashback. We arrive at the airport via a free military shuttle from Yongsan garrison and have plenty of time to spare before Mom and Dad's flight lands. This allows us to have lunch at a well-known fast-food burger-eatery that sports two yellow arches. Most American restaurants, when they go international, will take on the flavors of the host country. So it is no surprise the menu offerings here are quite different from those in the States. Celia has the *bulgogi* burger and I have the shrimp burger. After sampling each other's sandwich, we agree both were quite tasty.

Mom and Dad's plane lands earlier than scheduled so we miss their disembarkment. In the event just such a thing should happen, we have preplanned a meeting place. However, Celia begins to worry that something may have happened or that maybe they missed their flight, so we go in search of them. We traverse the building from end to end thrice. Did I mention the interior of Inchon is vast? Halfway into our fourth round we spot them. It has been years since Mom and Dad last traveled overseas on an airplane and I marvel at how spry they appear after the 14 hours it took to get here. The reason we could not find them earlier is because they were with airport officials arranging to have 3 pieces of lost luggage found and delivered to our address. They have been assured the luggage will be delivered in two days.

Welcome to Korea, Mom and Dad!

Okay, now comes the decision of how best to get back to the Yongsan garrison. We have four options which Celia, Mom, and Dad weigh. The first option is to take the free shuttle back, but it will not leave for at least another 45 minutes ($0). Do we want to wait 45 minutes? Option two is catch a taxi to Kempo where we could then take the subway to Itaewon and from there walk the mile to our house ($5). Walk a mile? What is option three? The third option involves taking a Korean taxi. Korean taxis are not allowed onto post so a ½-mile walk is then required to reach our house ($35). Hmm…There is walking here too. What's our fourth option? The fourth option, the one that is chosen, is to take an AAFES (Army and Air Force Exchange Service) taxi that will deliver us to the front door of our house ($50). Fifty dollars and well worth it.

Mom and Dad enter the taxi and immediately receive special treatment, this will continue throughout their stay. Our driver, a jovial Korean man, puts on his "tour guide" cap. He gestures to the landscape and explains to Mom and Dad, using very good English, items of interest. He is really nice and works hard for his tip, which we are very happy to give.

The following day is a "Lazy-day", which gives Mom and Dad a chance to recuperate. The first week we have them to ourselves, the second week we join the organized tour group. So much happens during their stay. This letter will be a thick tome if I try to describe everything we see and do. So I will use just a few sheets to highlight some of our activities during our first week together, like our outing to Itaewon.

Itaewon-dong (*Dong* translates to mean a street, a block, or a village. In this case it most likely means block, Itaewon-block.) is a large shopping district that has found popularity with the natives and with foreigners. In Itaewon one can purchase genuine articles as well as genuine imitation articles for relatively low prices. The district is just a stone's throw from Yongsan garrison. Because of its eclectic array of goods, we feel it's a good place to take Mom and Dad so they might be introduced to the touch, sights, smells, sounds, and tastes that flavor Korean culture. About 20 yards into the district, Mom experiences the touch of Korean culture.

She is strolling along and listening intently to Celia's dissertations on the various objects we encounter, when all of a sudden she feels something vibrating her shoulder. "OH!" she exclaims in alarm, while dipping her shoulder away from the vibrating object. She then twists around and eyes a grinning Korean man, around middle age, brandishing a small vibrating massager. He is obviously eager to show, by means of demonstration, how his motorized machinery manipulates and mellows muscles. Mom is having none of it. She smiles politely, turns to continue on her way, and the humming hand rests upon her shoulder for a second time. "OH!" she exclaims again. This time she not only dips her shoulder, but she also quickens her stride. A moment later she is executing an easy trot with the undaunted massage-merchant in hot pursuit.

Dad and Celia deeming the situation harmless, wear amused smiles. I, on the other hand, laugh openly (forgive me). It is the funniest thing I have seen all day. The scene reminds me of the silent era comedy skits of Charlie Chaplin and Harold Lloyd.

Eventually Mom travels beyond the border of the merchant's "selling-zone". The merchant has missed a sale. Grinning sheepishly he gives up the chase. I wipe moisture from my eyes as Mom catches her breath.

The goods sold in the Itaewon shops spill onto the sidewalks. It makes for cramped walking and progress cannot be made without brushing against humanity and/or goods. A tailor grabs my elbow and tries to guide me into his shop to be fitted for a suit. I assure him I already have a tailor. Reluctantly he lets go, pressing his business card into my hand. Leather purses are dangled in front of Celia's face and socks are thrust towards Dad. As you can see the shopkeepers here are quite aggressive. They have to be with so much competition in the vicinity. There really are some great bargains to be found here; by bargains I mean quality-manufactured goods for decent and outrageously low prices. However, you have to be a shrewd buyer. Better yet, be a shrewd buyer who goes to Itaewon with a Korean friend, they will lose face if they do not get you the best deal, and face is not a thing to lose in Korea. Having disclosed all of this, remember this outing is only a way to acquaint Mom and Dad with the area.

No matter where you are in Itaewon, local food is generally good and you will have a lot of establishments to choose from. At one such place we have *Bibimbap* (B's are often interchanged with P's when pronouncing Korean words, but for some reason "Pipimpap" doesn't sound as tasty.) *Bibimbap* is rice, vegetables (bell-flower root, bracken, bean sprouts, spinach, cucumber), sesame seed oil, red pepper paste, topped with a little bit of shredded beef and a raw egg all served steaming hot in a stoneware bowl. The whole dish is stirred together and the heat from the bowl cooks the egg quickly. Delicious!

Celia cannot resist making a purchase in Itaewon from a shop selling bronze castings of animals. The object that lures her in is a large bronze casting of an egg-shaped goldfish. I admire her designer's eye, for the piece is well crafted, whimsical, and will look good in our house or garden. Celia even takes the time to haggle a bit over the price, and is rewarded with a discount. I think it is fortunate that Mom and Dad have the opportunity to see their daughter with her shoppers-face on.   I am sure it is something they have never seen before. Unfortunately for Mom, the shop is situated next to the massage-merchant. As we exit the store the merchant espies Mom, Mom espies the merchant, and their fox and hound routine again amuses me.

Of course, we have to take Mom and Dad to the Dragon Hill Lodge (DHL). The DHL is a 394-room high-rise hotel situated on Yongsan Garrison. It also holds a casino, which has many enthusiastic supporters. No, we don't intend Mom and Dad to shake the hand of the "one-armed-bandit" (slot machine), but we do want them to see what the lodge offers. One can buy quality diamonds, emeralds, rubies, sapphires, other precious and semi-precious stones, gold and silver. If the Dragon Hill shops don't have what you are looking for, they can order it for you.   After a general tour of the building, its grounds, clubs, ballroom, shops, eateries, bank, and other amenities, we decide to eat pizza and salad at the lodge's Primo restaurant. Tomorrow we will eat Korean fare again, Dad's already hooked.

South Korea hosted the 1988 World Olympics and one of the "must see" places is their Olympic Park, with its unique display of sculptures formed by various artists. For this outing the subway is our best mode of transport. The car we enter is somewhat crowded. The moment Mom and

Dad set foot into it, two seated individuals, both junior in age to Mom and Dad, rocket to their feet and offer-up their seats. This is another special treatment they will enjoy by virtue of their having white hair on their heads. "White hairs", as they are called in Korea, are viewed with awe as wise, living treasures who are to be treated with honor and respect. "Here, here!" All right, so we take the line 4 subway from Ichon to Sadang and transfer to line 2 for Jamsil and disembark at Lotte World. Well... that is the plan, but somehow we get lost. Okay, wait, that is not entirely true; we get off at the wrong platform. Celia is a champion chart construer and if it is on a map she can find it (No... she is not making me write this, she really is good). So for whatever reason, Lotte World isn't on our map. The neighborhood map is of no aid to us either. However, several helpful Koreans notice our bewildered looks as we survey our map and they come to our rescue. Once they discern our dilemma, we are literally led by the hand to our destination.

In a Lotte world restaurant we order a dish for four using the native tongue. The dish the natives bring us is stomach, tripe to be exact...a cow's stomach. Wait a minute; let me see that menu again... A large platter of raw tripe, mushrooms, and an egg along with a one-burner propane stove is brought to our table. As we watch the cooking, we are served hot and mild *kim chi*. *Kim chi* is salted, pickled or fermented vegetables. We receive twelve different *kim chi* dishes, (spinach, cucumber, thinly sliced radish, cubed radish, string beans, bean sprouts, lotus root, cabbage, squash, potato, turnip, lettuce). We get rice also. Eat up

Dad! The total cost is 34,000W, just over twenty dollars U.S. at the current exchange rate.

A USO Tour we sign up for will take us to Kangwhado Island. Fifty kilometers later our tour guides, John and John, are explaining to us the historical significance of the Kangwasong fort[7] where the Koreans defended the Inchon harbor from the French and Americans circa 1871. The terrain is hilly with an excellent overlook onto the strait. Situated in nearby fields are vast quantities of red peppers, wild sesame, sugarcane, and melons. The rice paddies have been harvested already. Very picturesque. Onward to the Buddhist temple.

One cannot tour Korea without visiting at least one Buddhist temple. I will venture to say; having been to several, that one need only see one. Most temples in the countryside are on hills or mountaintops and are accessed by looong flights of stone stairs. I suppose this climb is a similitude of a pilgrimage. Upon reaching the top of the stairs we encounter an ancient well into which one can toss pre-written prayers purchased from the monks' store. Hmmm. The temple itself is fascinating and colorful with its beautifully restored ancient motifs and architecture. Within, one can truly get a feeling of stepping into the past. Mom says that while she was in the temple, she felt a great sense of peace and tranquility. Dad took pictures.

Crammed around the temple are shops where monks and non-monks peddle their wares. Everything from prayer beads and lucky prayer papers, to food and drinks can be purchased. We succumb to a platter of *bulgogi* (thinly sliced, marinated and grilled beef) for lunch. This was served with roasted garlic cloves, lettuce, barley water, and *kim chi*. I'm a bit surprised; Dad just loves *kim chi*, even though it makes him sweat. With full bellies we forge forward to the ginseng and bamboo market, and the opportunity to buy ginseng and bamboo items.

Ginseng means man-root, a description that denotes the root's resemblance to the humanoid form. Also known as *insam*, you can find this root, usually steeping in syrup or other fluid, throughout shops in Korea. It is purported to have desirable tonic qualities and has been used for centuries to treat all sorts of ailments from diabetes to cancer and most things in between. Its flavor is an acquired taste. Dad bought ginseng candies and two bamboo hats.

Insa-dong is the place to go for antiques, if you don't mind paying the proverbial arm and leg. It is lined with art galleries, small shops, restaurants, and teahouses. We stroll Insa-dong for a while before eating *mandu kuk* (dumpling soup) made by an 83-year young shop owner, and spending some time in a teahouse drinking fruit teas. The teahouse is decorated with paintings, old farm tools, and it has a recreated thatched-roof rest pavilion of the type Korean farmers use. Mom and I have plum tea, Dad has *jujube* tea (a fruit which resembles a date, but tastes slightly apple-like), and Celia has citron tea (a citrus fruit marmalade stirred into hot water).

For a brunch we take Mom and Dad to dine at the Hartell House, the Commander in Chief's mess. It serves the commanding generals of the United Nations Command, ROK (Republic of Korea)/US Combined Forces Command, United States Forces Korea and Eighth U.S. Army. Whew! I have had the privilege to eat here many times. The food is scrumptious, but the service is slooow. I always have something to eat at home before going to a function being held at the Hartell House. A word to the wise. Also, the Hartell House is great if you like baked potatoes, for a five pound spud is served with every dish. Well, that is not exactly true; it's more like two pounds. Okay...I'll just say it's big, really big.

There are so many shopping districts in Korea. Seoul was established circa 1398, and Namdaemun is its oldest shopping district. Namdaemun (Great South Gate) market is a warren of tiny shops numbering about 1000 on a miniscule ten acres. Squeezed-together describes the proximity of street vendors and shops in this market area. Here one can find specialty shops that carry only socks, or gloves, fish, men's underwear, etc. We halt at a street vendor's stand for three cups of coffee, one of tea, and some fried doughnuts. The hot liquid is served in 4-ounce waxed cardboard cups. Koreans traditionally serve a cup half filled or half empty if you will. It is considered a polite amount; any more could be seen as an insult. So we savor our 2 ounces of fluid and sip it slowly. One cannot complain though, at a total price of 3000 won (about $2.90) it's still a bargain. Namdaemun may be the oldest market in Seoul, but Myong-dong is the trendiest.

We want to show Mom and Dad the contrast of old and new markets so off we set for Myong-dong. There are over 300,000 square meters of shops selling food, garments, footwear, purses, makeup, and many accessories. It is also a site for frequent demonstrations by university students, which often get rowdy. However, nothing like that is on tap for today. So we have a nice day to browse and shop. Subways run beneath the district and vendors cram the station's halls and platform. A vendor here is selling old vinyl albums and we spot a "Porgy and Bess" soundtrack like one Mom has. Dorothy Dandridge sings on this album, which is Celia's favorite version. It's in pristine condition. Unbelievable! Cost? 7000 won ($6.50 or there about). Myong-dong has a Seattle's Best Coffee place, which has plate-glass windows and is situated such that we can sit and gaze down upon passing humanity. Celia orders for us in Korean. Dad has steamed milk; I have grape juice, while Mom and Celia split a white chocolate mocha. It is here Celia and I have our first-ever scones, which are similar to teacakes. Later we stop for dinner. Mom has fried *mandu* (dumplings), and Celia cold beef noodles. What did Dad and I have? I have no idea, but boy was it good! This is a fine cap to an enjoyable and enlightening week. Next week we will all join the Korea Reunion Tour group.

Korean Proverb

One near ink gets black.
If you stand near the fire, you can get burned.

An-nyeong! (Hi!)   15 Dec 01

It's a blast having Celia's parents (Mom and Dad) with us in Korea for two whole weeks! It's the beginning of the second week and Mom and Dad are still riding high with excitement. Celia and I are so glad they are, because today starts a week of touring with the Korea Reunion Tour group.

We call for a taxi which takes us to the Sheraton Walker Hotel located on the east side of Seoul. It sits on a hill overlooking the Han River, which flows through the center of Seoul. The hotel is considered to be a 5-star hotel or as the Koreans call it, a super deluxe. We are greeted by men in top hats and distinctive gray uniforms. The sign-in procedure is very organized and, in no time at all, we have our room cards. Our rooms, which are on the 10th floor, are comfortable and have lots of extra comfort items (slippers, thick robes, coffee maker, etc.). When I try the television it does not work, but that is no problem. It will be exchanged while we are at dinner. Oh yeah that's right, dinner. We had better iron our clothes, get dressed and go down to the Banquet Hall before all of the food is gone.

It seems I need not have worried about missing out on the food at this Welcome Dinner. There are buffet tables arranged in the shape of a large U, and they are just loaded with all manner of scrumptious items. Korean, Japanese, and Western fare is available as are fruits, tarts, strudels, cheese cakes and other dessert items. Celia and Mom decorate their plates with small samples of various tasty tidbits. Dad and I load our plates with everything within reach and we go for seconds, thirds, fourths... At some point during the dinner the Public Affairs Office of United States Forces Korea gives an overview briefing about Korean and American involvement in setting up all of this. A few hours later we waddle to our rooms for a restful night's sleep. The sleep is restful, but short.

At zero dark four thirty hours, a bugle is blown, not really a bugle, but it is time to get up. Yawn... Breakfast is at 0600 hours. 0600? Wait a minute, let me see that itinerary again. Yeah...it's 0600. We get moving and make it to the buffet-style breakfast in plenty of time to fill our bellies. Many hours will tick by before we eat again.

The tour bus arrives and we load up to visit Panmunjon, the Joint Security Area (JSA), also known as the DMZ (Demilitarized Zone). During the ride we get to meet more of our tour group, which includes the commanding general's wife. She is a nice, immediately likeable person who is not shy when it comes to having fun. That's good. Her belly-laugh is genuine and we hear it frequently throughout the trip. She and Dad get along like old pals.

The DMZ is where North and South Korea meet and it is a place of high tension. A confrontation could happen here at any moment. It could manifest because a North Korean bolts for the South Korean side of the border, or because of a miscommunication between the border guards. The DMZ has become a popular tourist stop, but make no mistake, it is a dangerous place and will be so until the two halves of Korea can live together in harmony. An Army Specialist gives us a short JSA briefing before leading us on a walking tour of the grounds. He then takes us into a special conference building which is the only place where we can actually step into North Korea, which I do. When we exit the building, we notice a North Korean tour group staring forlornly at the south side. They look a little thin and I feel a slight pang of guilt, for our next stop is a buffet luncheon at Camp Bonifas.

In short order, another meal under our belts, we're off to Changdok Palace[8]. We arrive just in time to witness the changing of the guard, a colorful ceremony accompanied by the boom of a seven-foot drum. Changdok Palace was constructed in 1405 as an auxiliary palace and occupies around 110 acres of Seoul. This lavish palace has a garden called "The Secret Garden" that was strictly reserved as a place for the royal family to relax. I'll bet never in their wildest dreams did the royal family imagine that one day we would be climbing their stairs, sauntering along their stone walkways, crunching royal gravel with our western heels, and promenading past their precious pavilions. The pavilions in this garden, beautifully set among hills, are architectural works of art. Being surrounded by shaped evergreens and large trees further enhances their attractiveness. Some of the trees are over 700 years old. We enjoy the several lily-padded ponds sporting central islands, which offer serene settings for meditation.

Back at the hotel, we enjoy a reception of hors d'oeuvres before partaking in another magnificent banquet.

After the meal, a Korean dancer entertains us. She does a widow's dance, a traditional dance a widow performs in an effort to reclaim the spirit of her deceased husband. This economical dance is a wonder to watch. She dips, waves her arms gracefully, tilts her head every which way, and glides across the stage in a colorful costume which sports sleeves so long they sweep the floor.

Next on the program is a child prodigy, a cherubic Korean boy of 5 or 6 years of age. He beats an array of traditional and non-traditional drums of various sizes thereby creating complex rhythms that wow the audience. He may be young, but he knows he is good and he twitches, jerks, shakes, and gyrates to the beats ad infinitum.

It's another morning, and on tap for today is a Korean Folk Village. There are several folk villages in and around Seoul. The one we visit is the largest. The village allows us to gaze upon and partake in the traditions of Korea's past and it houses several of Korea's Living Treasures. Living Treasures are the ancient Korean artisans who yet live and breathe and are able to continue toiling at their profession. The 90-year-old rope maker, the 80-something sandal maker, and the 90-some-odd potter are a few of the treasures we meet. Since it is harvest time, there are numerous flat baskets of hot peppers and persimmons drying in the sun. Braided corncobs, onions, and garlic hang from rafters.

Dad signs a child's autograph book, and is then inundated with requests from other children. Dad loves to oblige, he really becomes quite lively when interacting with children.   Later Mom and Dad get to watch Chinese acrobats, Korean folk dancers, and a traditional wedding ceremony.   They are definitely ready to eat when we make for the folk village's *Bulgogi* restaurant.

We do not head back to the hotel when our meal is over, instead we hop on the bus for a 5-hour ride to Kwangju.   The Kolon Hotel, another 5-star/super deluxe hotel, is to be our residence for the night.   Can you believe our television does not work in this room either?   A replacement will be installed while we are at dinner.   At least the hotels are consistent.   Dinner is a fabulous buffet and an ice sculpture of an eagle serves as a focal piece.   These buffets are an excellent way to get food to a lot of people in a hurry.   Also, diners can easily pick the items and amounts they desire.   While we eat, a male pianist and female songstress regale us with American hits, sung in English, from the 1970's.   Next we get to watch a video from the Korean Tourism Organization.

We were allowed an extra hour of sleep this morning so we feel refreshed and ready to go touring, after breakfast of course.   Today Bulguksa, a mountain Buddhist temple, is our first destination.   We negotiate the usual stone stairs before hiking a long dirt road that winds along the edge of the mountain.   Mom notices an elderly lady, one of our group members, who keeps straying dangerously close to the edge of the path.   There is no guardrail and the drop-off is several hundred feet.   To avoid a tragedy I interpose myself between her and the edge.   The lady is not unwise, she knows what I am doing.   She thanks me and says her sugar is a little low. She then strikes up a conversation which sees us to the temple. The attractive temple, built c.528 AD, is secluded among tall trees and faces east so that it might catch the first rays of the rising sun. From this vantage point we can enjoy a stunning view of mountains marching to the sea some thirty miles away. On site azaleas, evergreen pines, and deciduous trees set off a large pond, a perfect place for reflective moments.

There are seven national treasures at this location (Numbers 20, 21, 22, 23, 26, 27, and 61). Treasure No.20 and No.21 are two stone pagodas, treasure No.22 is the Lotus Flower Bridge, No.23 is the Blue Cloud Bridge. Treasure No.26, a seated 6-foot gilt-bronze Vairocana Buddha statue, is housed within a temple. A nun and a priest are tending the temple's interior and offering up prayers. There are signs asking people to resist the urge to take photos, they are useless. Click. "I must please ask," says the guide, - Click, Click - "that no pictures are taken while inside." Click, click, click, click, click. See what I mean?

National treasure No.27 is the seated gilt-bronze Amitabha Buddha statue, and No.61 is the 6½-foot sarira pagoda, a container for the relics or remains of famous priests or royalty. It looks akin to a stone lantern and is said to contain the remains of eight priests and a queen.

In one of the wooden pagodas is a 5-foot colorfully painted drum mounted on the back of a wooden turtle. The drum is used to call forth spirits. An 8-foot long, hollow, painted, wooden fish is also used as a drum by Buddhist disciples to signal the start and end of a meditation session.

Working our way down the steep, uneven, crumbling stone stairs is a tricky procedure and our whole attention is given to it. It's quite taxing. When we reach the parking lot, but before we can catch our breath, Dad and I are encircled by school children waving autograph books. One would think we are celebrities. This signing session delays our boarding the bus. Our tour guide is perturbed and informs the group that from now on the last person on the bus will have to sing a song. Since Dad is usually the last to board the bus, I put in my request early. I want to hear him sing "Turkey in the Straw", dancing is optional as space on the bus is limited. Dad laughs, but I think my chances are pretty good that after the next stop he'll be crooning on the microphone.

A museum is our next stop. As usual, children thrust their autograph books at Dad and me. This gives everyone a chance to load the bus, making us the last two. So we are conversing quietly and strolling toward the bus when all of a sudden Dad takes off, sprinting the last 15 or so yards to the bus. I've never before seen him move so fast. I'm so astonished, all I can do is watch him grin as he boards the bus. Ooo! So now I have to sing. "Sing "Turkey in the Straw"!" Dad requests. Har-de-har. Celia is nice enough to sing with me and we sing a song titled "By and By". She later sings "My Favorite Things". Ah, the voice of an angel.

The thousand-year-old hill tombs of the *Shilla* Dynasty[9] located in Tumuli Park are something to see. The 23 tombs, which house *Shilla* period royalty, are gigantic grassy mounds (70+ feet high?) with an understructure of stone blocks that allow for the actual tomb space. The crypts vary in height and girth, denoting the importance of the entombed. One of the structures, known as the Flying-horse tomb, is now a museum and displayed are dioramas, items of gold, earthenware objects, jewelry, clothes, and other artifacts. Also at this park is the oldest known astronomical observatory, a bottle-shaped construct built in the 7th century.

If I may make two travel suggestions concerning touring via a bus, never miss an opportunity to visit the latrine and always drink sparingly. Tour bus drivers must not have bladders, because they are notorious for not wanting to make unscheduled stops to let passengers answer the calls of nature. Our first rest stop as we make our way back to Seoul is over two hours away, so it is no surprise that many in our group, those who topped off their fluid level at breakfast, resemble contortionists as they try to contain their water. Tempers are hot and feet fleet when we finally roll up to a rest area that has a market, food stalls, and craft shops. By this time Celia and I are exceedingly thirsty and we buy a variety of drinks in 250ml containers. The formerly contorted, relieved and resituated within the bus, look upon us with sympathetic and knowing looks as we swill our purchases.

Once we are back in Seoul, we enjoy our last luncheon at the Sheraton Walker before reloading the bus for the trip to Yongsan garrison. It takes almost an hour to get through Yongsan's entry gate due to organized protests and heightened security procedures. Never a dull moment.

The day is warm and clear. Rather than stay on post, we call a taxi and head to Seoul Tower. The taxi driver careens through traffic and finally up a road to the mountain top site of Namsan (South Mountain) Park in which stands the tower. We are driven quite a distance up, but the last leg of the journey will be covered on foot via stairs or a very steep asphalt path. The taxi driver lets us out at the path. Leaning forward about 30 degrees and giving our calves a killer workout, we make our way to the tower.

Within the tower, the uniformed maidens greet us warmly before ushering us into an elevator. It has been growing steadily darker during our journey, and darkness reigns by the time we reach the tower's first observation deck (there are two). From here the traffic on the main roads appears to be ribbons of white and red lights. The bright lights of Seoul radiate out for several miles and then end abruptly where the countryside begins. It is a very dramatic view and it imparts the impression of being on an island. Upon leaving the tower we opt to tread the distance to the base of the mountain park, singing all the way. Once outside the park, we catch a cab and enjoy a wild ride through narrow back streets lined with shops and clubs. It's been a fun evening, and sadly the last evening before Mom and Dad fly home.

There is a lump in my throat as I bid farewell to Mom and Dad, even though it will be less than a year before I see them again. I have grown close to them over the years and, because they are so keen to travel to the many places we are stationed, have had a lot of interaction with them. The Korea Reunion Tour was a good way for us to get together and enjoy some of the many attractions Korea has to offer.

Until next time,

An-nyeong-he-kaseyo (Go in peace)

Korean Cultural Tip

Koreans politely refuse an offer at least two or three times before accepting it. If you wish to give a gift to a Korean, do not be surprised if at first the gift is declined. Offer the gift several more times.

If you are hosting a dinner and offer your guest more to eat, follow the same procedure. Another clue for a meal host is a clean plate which indicates the person is still hungry and willing to have more.

Korean Proverb

Even a fish would not get into trouble if it kept its mouth shut.
A closed mouth catches no flies.

Greeting All!   7 Jan 02

"What is your name? How old are you? Does your wife have a job? What does she do? How old is she? How many children do you have?" These are questions Korean women over the age of 39 will ask me. They are quite bold.

Whoa! Wait a minute. That's a lot of information you are asking for...I've only just met you (No... I'm not saying this out loud. I'm only thinking it.). The above questions are what I have had to get comfortable hearing and answering. I am finding it is just the way some Korean women approach Americans. I say Americans, because I have no idea if they do this amongst themselves as well. Celia is asked these questions concerning me and I will generally get these types of hard, fast questions if we are in the company of two or more Korean women. The exception is if we are at a social function, then only one Korean lady is required.

Okay, so let's say that name, job, and age have been divulged. I don't let the ladies off the hook; I ask them for the same information they have asked of me. Hmm, now they get all coy. "What is your name?" I ask. I wait for an answer before asking. "How old are you?" (Korean women can look quite youthful into their 60's. Ask them about their fountain of youth, and they will tell you it is in the *kim chi*. There. You didn't think I was going to write a letter concerning Korea without mentioning *kim chi* did you?)

"What does your husband do for a living?" I continue. "How old is he? Do you work as well? How old are your children?"

Well, my questions are slightly different. I was not asked what I do for a living, but I put the question to them. This is because ten years or so ago, it was traditional that Korean women not work outside the home. However, that has changed and many women now embrace the opportunity to earn a wage doing something they find interesting. Also, I imagine they have a greater sense of independence. Even so, many Korean women will not initiate a conversation about their job, but once you ask them about it they will happily convey all you wish to know. All of that aside, the really important information the Korean women (usually 40 and over) want to hear is the answer to how many children you have.

A Korean woman, when she gets married, is expected to have at least one child and stay at home to raise her offspring. This is her main job and anything else that she decides to partake in is considered extracurricular. Okay, by today's standards this is an archaic way of thinking, but in women 40 and over it persists. So when they ask how many children I have and I say none, the conversation dwindles to an uncomfortable silence. They are done with me. But wait! All is not lost.

"How old are your children?" I ask, genuinely interested. I make the bold assumption they have children and luckily so far I have not been wrong. Upon hearing this question, the "conversation curtain" is lifted, the sun beams upon their radiant faces, and we happily converse about their children for hours.

Korean women can be extremely nice, cheerful, courteous, and quite shy. However, I have been witness to their flip side too. Oh boy...I would not want be on the receiving end of their wrath. It does not take much for them to get themselves worked up, but it takes some doing to calm them down. Having said that, with few exceptions the Korean women Celia and I meet are very, very gracious. We are certain that in the time we have been here, we have forged friendships that will last a lifetime.

When I was growing up, my mother was the backbone and the glue that held my family together. I can only chalk it up to her maternal instinct. I see the same thing in South Korean women. They are the backbone and glue of South Korea. It's a fact. It is the same with the women in the United States and other countries. Some day women around the world will come to realize their worth and what they are truly capable of doing and I believe things will be quite different. I hope I am around to see it.

Love to you!

Korean Proverb

While two are eating, one could die and the other not know.
When eating delicious food, we are conscious of nothing else.

Hey All,   22 Mar 02

It's good to know the world is round, otherwise you may think I've fallen over the edge. No, there just hasn't been much to write about lately. Unless you count the dysentery outbreak.

There was a dysentery outbreak here. We weren't affected by this intestinal disease, but hundreds were, mostly Koreans. The disease was spread through a popular food dish called *kimbap*. You may remember *kimbap* as vegetables, meat, and rice all rolled up in a thin sheet of dried seaweed. The *kimbap* "factory" created a culinary calamity by not following good hygiene practices. I put the word "factory" in quotations because I'm using the term loosely, very loosely! Korea is truly the land of the cottage industry. Here, a factory can consist of no more than a ninety-year old woman and her great-granddaughter, putting meals together in their home kitchen and selling them to the public. There does not seem to be any real health standards for food production. Contaminants are in the Korean tap water system as well.

I quote, "Of the 32 water purification plants in 19 cities and counties subject to inspection, officials said 65 were contaminated with excessive levels of hazardous materials." How does one get 65 from 32? Anyway, by cracking open the pipes, inspectors are finding the pipes are almost blocked by sediment and metal deposits. A host of bacteria romp in the pipes, there are high levels of iron, copper, zinc, manganese, and chlorine ions. Whew! All this writing about water is making me thirsty! Fortunately, once again we are insulated from harm, as the military's water supply is not affected...I think. I can pump all the iron I want in the gym, I don't need it pumped into my water glass as well.

Korea is once again engulfed in a fog of sand. It is unaffectionately known as *Hwangsa*, or yellow sand (or wind). These annual storms, born from the Gobi desert, can billow sand 7 to 8 kilometers high! This year's sandy curtain is definitely thicker than last year's. Whenever Celia and I go outside, we cover mouth and nose with a winter scarf. Our eyes have to suffer the sand blasting.

> Let me say this, I'll try to be brief
> The sand storm here's beyond belief
> It sure makes me seethe
> To have grit on my teeth
> Only indoors can I find relief

Things are heating up over here and it will be best to be elsewhere when the fertilizer hits the propeller. We will take with us some great pictures, many good memories, and the friendship of the special people we've met during our tour.

Celia finally received orders for her next assignment. We have been actively searching for our next house, and have quite a number of prospects. This Saturday (23 Mar 02), we fly to Virginia. We will meet with a realtor and house hunt. We can really only stay for as long as it takes us to find the home we want and close the deal. So, we probably won't get to see everybody during this trip. However, after July 25th we should again be State side. Let the visiting begin! Looking forward to seeing you!!

Korean Proverb

Licking the outside of a watermelon.
Scratching the surface.

Spain

Ola! (Hi!)

Here's the letter I promised you about our trip to Spain.

There was a time when Celia and I were both on military assignments in Augsburg, Germany. Augsburg is a beautiful place with a history of over 2000 years. It is also a hub from which one might travel to other European lands relatively quickly and easily. For us, traveling to such places would be very easy indeed.

The military has a Morale, Welfare, and Recreation Office (MWR), which schedules wallet-friendly global trips for soldiers, government civilians, and their family members. Most of the people we talked to who had been on MWR trips had nothing but good stories to tell. We were encouraged. Celia and I like visiting new places, so when we heard MWR was offering a trip to Spain with five-star treatments for only a few hundred dollars, we signed up with high anticipation of a great experience. Not long after we signed up the trip was canceled. Before we could get our money back the trip was on again. This happened three times. Only in hindsight can I say it was a forewarning that the trip would be fraught with troubles...

It is the morning of our departure and the bus is three hours late. Our luggage doubles as seats while we impatiently wait with an assemblage for what we were promised would be a top-of-the-line, luxury-liner bus, complete with air-conditioning, roomy, reclining, velvet-covered seats with headphone jacks in the armrests, a lavish latrine, and an advanced suspension system that will give us a "riding-on-air" experience. The coach that finally comes rumbling down the street towards us sets the tone for the whole of the trip to Spain. Our jaws drop as we view an ancient yellow school bus. The bus is belching thick black smoke and threatening to stall at any moment. "What is THIS?" yells most of the assemblage as they leap to their feet. Angry shouts of disappointment and streams of torrid curses warm the morning air.

Another half hour is lost to a discussion by a number of the outraged travelers concerning the transportation they had been promised. What are we to do, refuse to go? Yes, we could do that and probably not get a refund. There's no use yelling at the driver, he only drives what he is given. Sigh. Feeling cheated, and with quite a few people still muttering curses, we load the bus. The luggage is crammed into the seating compartment with us and there is no way to stretch out our legs. Once underway, we feel every cobblestone, crack, and imperfection the roads have to offer. Straight-backed, worn, leather seats ensure our ride is supremely uncomfortable; there isn't even an armrest.

The rear of the bus has been outfitted with a makeshift latrine, minus the all-important exhaust (extraction) fan. Unbelievable! More than half of the bus's occupants are in need of the facilities and a line forms in the aisle. With each opening of the door the foul smell of excrement billows through the seating area. Good GOSH! Windows are hastily opened, but for some reason the gut-wrenching aroma intensifies before exiting the bus. We are not yet 20 kilometers from Augsburg, with hundreds of kilometers to go, when the toilet refuses to flush. There are a great many riders still needing relief. Each in turn makes his deposit and the liabilities pile up (Sorry to go on ad nauseam, but do you feel my pain?). Eventually, even those in dire need of relief refuse to enter the chocked chamber and demands are directed at the driver to find suitable roadside facilities. The driver grumbles about the time schedule and says, "We will stop when we reach France." However, amid angry protests from his fares, he complies and we stop briefly. At this point nothing can be done about the bus latrine. Its door is taped shut with duct tape, for it otherwise refuses to stay closed. Thankfully, the bus has aired somewhat by the time we load up to continue our journey.

It's a gloomy day for traveling, it is made even more so by the recent revelations. The weather is sweltering and very humid. That the bus is not equipped with the promised air-conditioning is no surprise. Even though the roof vents are fully open and the few windows that can be opened are down, the seating compartment is a hotbox. Celia has beads of perspiration on her upper lip. I'm sweating copiously and the back of my wet shirt is plastered against the seat.

It has been threatening to rain all morning. Heralded by a crack of thunder, the blackened clouds, unable to contain their moisture any longer, release a deluge. Water pours into the bus. Vents and windows are closed, the windows fog, the inside temperature rises, and we are treated to a steam bath before the vents are thrown open again. Water pours into the bus. In a very short time there is about an inch of water covering the floor. Using the soles of our shoes we try to squeegee the water to the front of the bus and out the door. It is useless. Eventually, when there are several inches of water on the floor it flows out of the bus of its own accord. You may as well know right now that water is to figure largely throughout this trip. Soaked and sullen, we travel in steamy silence into the night.

Our stop in France does nothing to improve the traveling spirit. Tired, hot, and hungry we disembark from the bus, stretch, and make our way to a restaurant. The food smells good and our mouths moisten. A moment later our mouths turn dry as the restaurant refuses to take our German Marks or American money. No one thought to bring French francs, being so close to the German border we assumed they would take marks. The restaurateur is crisp and rude. We reload the bus vowing to remember this little bit of French hospitality. I've never had the opportunity to visit France again, so this is the only memory I have of its people and country. Isn't that sad? It is a good thing to remember that we are all ambassadors (even if unofficial) of whatever country we're from, and we may only get one chance to make a good impression.

It's about midmorning when we arrive at Costa Brava, Spain, where our destination will be Lloret de Mar.

The rain has stopped, but newly eroded soil and large puddles of standing water are telltale signs that this area received a fair amount of rain. As the bus trundles into the city, large, grand hotels greet us. The buildings and sand are bright, as though angel-rays are beaming upon them (Angel-rays, you've probably seen them before; when rain clouds part and the rays of sunshine beam through in an inverted fan pattern). We press our faces against the windows and gawk. After the ride we've endured, this is like reaching the land of "Ahzz". So many fine-looking hotels are practically right on the beach. Ah, things are looking up! We are eager to check into our hotel and then stretch our legs on the beach. However, our bus continues through the city and into the dank, older portion of town. Here I see men weaving down the sidewalk and a few swilling liquid from bottles still in brown paper sacks. "Hey!" someone yells to the bus driver. "Turn the bus around; the good hotels are back that way!" There are "Yeahs" of agreement, but to no avail. Our driver continues to grind the gears as he coaxes the bus up steep and narrow roads that seem more akin to alleyways. We've left the land of "Ahzz" and entered the land of "Groans".

After a long time traversing the maze of roads, the bus comes to a stop and the driver sets the parking brake. Celia and I have no idea why we're stopping here. We hope it is just so the driver can get directions back to the beachfront hotels. The agitated passengers are getting angry and want to know why we have parked where there is no hotel in sight. Oh, but there is a hotel...or rather a Youth Hostel. A Youth Hostel is where basic accommodations are provided inexpensively to hiking youths. "Everybody off," pipes our driver, "we're here." "We're where?" I ask, angrily. However, the driver has already hopped off the bus and is entering the building where we are to stay. Everyone sits stunned for a moment before filing out resignedly.

"Look at that!" exclaims the first person off the bus. We look and see a forty-foot deep sinkhole right across from our hostel. Formerly, the hole must have been a parking lot for there is a jumble of cars at its bottom. A hastily erected fence of chain link keeps passersby from pitching headlong into the pit. We soon find that there is another large sinkhole nearby. It is in our hostel's roof!

Last night rain collected on the flat roof faster than it could drain. The subsequent weight became too much for the roof, which gave way and spilled enough water to soak the top three levels of the hostel (our three levels). Needless to say we now have no rooms, but are assured that every vacuum in the place is employed to suck up the water. For now we will wait in the lobby and enjoy a complimentary continental breakfast, which consists of Melba toast, butter, jam, mineral water, coffee, and tea. Hmm…let me see that brochure again and what it says about five star treatments.

> Once I read a brochure about Spain
> Of truth it held maybe a grain
> Great sights, it told me
> Five star luxury
> On my tour this was hidden, not plain

Four hours later, rooms become available for some passengers. Celia, I, and six others are the only ones without rooms. We are informed that we will be transported to another section of town for our accommodations. We pile into a van and off we go along the twisting streets. Our group is broken up into three hostels, with Celia and me being the last stop. The hostel is not very close to the beach but there is sand all over the floor of our room. There seems to be a perpetual party going on in the room right across from ours. College kids? We will stay in two other hostels before our time in Spain is up.

Although our group is scattered to the four corners of the town, there is an itinerary of activities for us to do everyday and the group is brought together for this. We partake of many activities, but for the sake of length and your patience I will only highlight a few. The first place we visit is a nightclub to watch flamenco dancing. Once seated, we are served a meal of roasted chicken, roasted potatoes, iced tea, and water. Delicious. When our empty plates are taken away, the floor in the center of the room, which has been kept clear, raises up to make a four-foot high stage. A family of flamenco dancers, an ageless mother and her three lovely daughters, soon populates the stage. The roof above them slides back to reveal the night sky. Whirling, stamping, and twisting to the strums from an accomplished acoustic guitarist, the dancers treat us to their energetic rendition of flamenco.

Another place we are taken, on a different day, is a mock medieval castle. Inside the building there is a small stadium outfitted with long tables and an oval of sand where jousting will take place. To make us feel like royalty, we are given paper crowns to wear. Fully armored jousters on horseback, performers of riding tricks, and sword duelists entertain us. During the joust, we are served a meal of roasted chicken, roasted potatoes, flagons of iced tea, and water. Again? (Yes, and we will have it twice more before we bid Spain farewell. Ay, *caramba*! I imagine Spain has a surplus of chicken and potatoes.) The knights are bedecked in green, white, black, blue, or red and we are encouraged to pick a knight to be our champion. Around mouthfuls of chicken and spuds we laugh, hoot, and holler to "egg on" our favorite, the red knight. He is eventually the overall winner. When the jousting is done we are herded to another part of the building to be serenaded by the Supremes, minus Diana Ross. They do a nice job, a cap to a most enjoyable evening.

The next day is a doozie. We are taken to a remote beach for a beach party, surf, sand, heat, and not an inch of shade. This is our environment for the next six hours. There is plenty of beer, which flows freely for those who wish to indulge. There are also beach-type games to play; games Celia forbids me to join just because the female players are topless. "Oh, are they? Hmph...I hadn't noticed, I'm too busy looking at you." So we play in the surf, or laugh and converse while lounging on the hot sand. At the end of the six hours Celia has her worst sunburn ever. Her skin is the hue of a boiled lobster shell. By the time we get back into our room, Celia has puffed up so much; her feet will not fit into her shoes. She is in some serious pain. Anywhere she wants or needs to go requires that I lift and carry her there. This is not how we envisioned we'd tour Spain. I search for and find an apothecary shop which sells me a sunburn remedy. Celia gets better in a surprisingly short period of time; it is well, for we are about to embark on a bus ride to Barcelona.

We travel in high style to Barcelona on a bus, which possesses all of the amenities our decrepit school bus lacks. Our female tour guide and male bus driver greet us warmly. The guide turns on a microphone and gives us a description of the day's agenda. That done, she sits down, forgets to turn off the "mike", and immediately starts an argument (in Spanish) with the driver, whom I assume is her boyfriend. It isn't long before she is weeping into the microphone (Oh joy...). At some point someone tells her the microphone is still on. She turns it off, but continues to weep and argue alternately until we reach Barcelona. Our guide looks at us through red-rimmed eyes and between sniffles she describes the passing sights. She is not having a good day. It gets worse. When we stop for a rest break our guide storms off the bus and has her hair blown into disarray by a strong wind. She is still trying to get control of the hair when she sits on a folding chair, which promptly gives way beneath her. As she plummets to the ground the wind whips her skirt up and over her head (censored). Celia and I rush over and help her to her feet. Poor thing, she is so embarrassed. Ahem. Some of the other sights we see include edifices by the late great architect, Antonio Gaudi. Most of his works are highly organic in their design, meaning there are none of the conventional corners or angles. For that reason I find them fascinating to look at, but too disturbing to desire one as my home.

Lunch today consists of roasted chicken, potatoes… just kidding. We are actually treated to a smorgasbord and we eat heartily. In the restaurant a huge, revolving, circular table allows us to easily choose from a vast array of food items. Here I have my first ever taste of paella and flan. The paella I chose of my own accord, but the flan I had shoved into my mouth by one of the females in our group after I told her I didn't think I'd like its texture (Ooo! Women are always shoving food into my mouth as though they think I am on the brink of starvation.). I still don't care much for flan.

Barcelona marks the closing of our stint in Spain. Tomorrow we will load up for the pleasure trip back to Augsburg. When I consider the price we paid for this trip, the accommodations, and the over-all menu, I think MWR owes us quite a few dollars change. However, despite the mishaps and misadventures, Celia and I have had a great time. We always do when we are together.

Until next time, *vaya con Dios, mi amigos*! (Go with God, my friends!)

Korean Cultural Tip

Office workers often take a nap at their desks after lunch. It is not uncommon to come across someone with his shirt or jacket removed and his head resting on his arms. If you are so desperate to get something done that you feel you must disturb him, cough politely and wait for him to put on his shirt or jacket. Then you can go ahead with your business.

Korean Proverb

East question, west answer.
When someone gives an answer unrelated to the question.

Dear All,   14 Jun 02

We were fortunate to have a wonderful realtor named Lydia. For almost two weeks she drove us to various parts of Northern Virginia to look at houses. In a short time she also became a friend. The real estate market in Virginia right now is a seller's market. This means that the seller can set a ridiculously high price for his house and still have people clamoring to buy it. After several disappointments, we finally found a charming house. It has three bedrooms, three and a half bathrooms, a full basement, and a two car garage, all situated on 2.33 acres. There is no landscaping to speak of, but we have already worked up a landscape design which includes plenty of flowers, trees, fruits, and vegetables. The house is neighbor to a thoroughbred horse ranch.

Our hotel during our stay was an Extended Stay America near Dulles Airport. The manager there was a friendly, generous, and well-spoken Palestinian. He frequently went out of his way to make our stay as comfortable as possible. When he found out we were military, he felt compelled to explain in detail why his countrymen engage in suicide bombing. We listened intently. He grew more impassioned as he spoke. It's still a terrible thing to do, but at least now we know the 'real' reason why they do it.

Our whole trip was peppered with strange surprises. I could write pages, and I will, telling you about our restaurant experiences during our two week foray in

Virginia. Our first day there, we decided to dine at the Macaroni Grill Restaurant. Here they serve, as an appetizer, freshly baked bread with a dish of olive oil and cracked pepper. Well, having received a steaming loaf, our waiter, Ben, cracked pepper into a dish and then reached for the magnum of olive oil on our table. But wait! Unbeknownst to Ben, the top is not screwed on. The oily bottle rocketed from his grip and crashed onto the dish. WHAM!! Pottery and pepper flew everywhere, and though the place was crowded, I was the only one who received a baptism of extra virgin olive oil! Restaurant activity ceased as pottery shards tinkled to a halt in various quadrants of the establishment. All eyes turned to our vermilion-faced waiter. I pretended not to notice that I was dripping with oil.

Another day, after spending all morning looking at houses, we decided to search for a place to have lunch. It was to be Lydia's treat. She took us to a place called the Tuscaro, an Italian dining facility (uh-oh, another Italian restaurant). The building was a restored 1800's grain mill, picturesque, with prices as high as its ceiling. Our waitress, a young lass, with a 1960's 'yeah man, cool, peace and love' disposition, sauntered over to our table. The table seated six, and as we were a party of three she began to remove the other place settings. A plate slipped from her hand and plummeted to the floor. "I'm having a bad day," she said. She jettisoned another plate and it rolled across the floor and under a table. "See?" she sighed. "I told you, I'm having a bad day. I'm going to go away for a while. I may be back, or I may not. Okay?" And she left. Lydia was livid! So to try to soothe her and help her see that these things happen, I told her the olive-oil story. Her reaction was akin to throwing gasoline on red hot coals. She was appalled by our initiation into Virginia hospitality. Then we heard a big CRASH! It was our waitress again, this time on the other side of the room. Finally, after a bit of Zen meditation, our waitress recovered enough to serve Celia a lamb sandwich and me a pastrami on rye. *Viva Italiana!*

Then there was the "Mom and Pop" eatery where the waitress lay on the table to take our order (I'm **not** making this up), and the musical meals at Bob Evans.

Of wait staff I have this to say
They drape me in the soup of the day
My repast they spoil
With a shower of oil
Being a spectacle's become my forté

We arrived safely back in Korea. This time we were able to leave the Inchon International Airport without incident. The last time we landed there, from our trip to Tokyo, Japan, we were involved in a police sting operation. Yeah, lots of excitement in Korea these days. Here's how it happened.

We had just exited the airport terminal and went in search of an AAFES taxi (Army and Air Force Exchange Services). AAFES taxis take American money and can deliver us to the door of our military housing. Korean taxis are not allowed on post. As we headed to the taxi stand, a

Korean taxi driver called to us from the shadows. "Pssst! You called for a taxi?"

Immediately, I had a vision of a man in a rumpled, tan trench coat trying to sell a 'genuine Rolex' for $20. In a word, shady. I told him, no, we did not call for a taxi. He kept looking around nervously and insisting that he would give us the best price. Finally, we struck a bargain and he walked with us across the street and bade us wait while he went to get his taxi. We had an uneasy feeling about the whole thing and just as we were about to retrace our steps, a Korean policeman came to us and asked what the man we were with had wanted. We told him and he asked us to follow him.

He took us to a spot just outside the airport terminal and asked us to please wait. He then made a call on his radio and police began to converge on the scene. Other Korean taxi drivers became alert and agitated. Several times the policeman came by to thank us for being so patient. Finally, our taxi driver showed up. He got out of his car, and was completely engulfed by the police as they arrested him. The policeman explained, "He is a very bad man, a renegade running an illegal taxi service. He has taken food from the mouths of honest, hard-working taxi drivers and their families." Yes, a very bad man indeed!

We will see Inchon again, soon, and for the last time, as we fly out of Korea. This is the time of year when there is an exodus of soldiers on their way to new assignments around the world. Every individual that is reassigned, is 'farewelled' by the people they worked with. These farewells can be held any number of places, but usually end in restaurants. A recent farewell was held at a place called Italianni's, (yep, this is how they spelled it) a Korean-run Italian restaurant. The food was good, just like an Italian chef may have made it. The place itself was of new construction and housed many progressive features.

Take their latrine for instance (yes, I know, I've spent a lot of time in the latrine in Korea), the latrine stalls have flat-screen televisions on both sides of the doors. It's the strangest thing though, all you get to see are commercials about the restaurant. Is that supposed to be an inducement to get busy? I guess it is for some.

Well, I only went in to wash my hands anyway. I banged the dispenser for soap, and a watery, blue liquid came out. I rubbed my hands together in a effort to produce a lather...nothing. I tried the dispenser again filling my cupped palm with blue elixir. Not the slightest hint of lather. Maybe, I thought, more money should have gone into quality soap instead of flat-screen televisions!

I became conscious of a Korean man (part of the wait staff) who had been watching my exertions from the corner of his eye. I looked down at my latherless hands and for the first time noticed a minty freshness in the air. Realization dawning, I glanced at the dispenser. On the top were small paper cups. You guessed it. Mouthwash. I had been trying to wash my hands with mouthwash. I reached for the 'real' soap, the Korean left, smiling broadly.

I had to pass the wait staff in order to get back to my seat. The staff looked at me and started grinning and tittering. The story had obviously spread rapidly. What are the Koreans going to do for entertainment when I leave?

Have a glorious day!!!

Fried Bean Curd (*Tubu Puch'im*)

A very simple dish to make is fried bean curd. Soybean curd does not have any flavor on its own, or at least not much, so the seasoning is very important. In addition to the method described below, you can also marinate the curd for a minute or two in the soy sauce before you start to cook it. The flavor permeates all the way through.

1 package firm tofu
3 T sesame oil
3 T soy sauce
5 small green onions cut in 1" lengths
1 t red pepper threads (or ½ t red pepper powder)
1/8 t black pepper
2 T sesame salt

1. Cut the bean curd into slices ¼" thick. Fry them in the oil over low heat until light brown on both sides.
2. Sprinkle with the rest of the ingredients and cook two more minutes on each side.

Korean Proverb

Shrimp's backs are broken when whales fight.
Little people get hurt when important people fight.

Dear All,   30 Jun 02

This will more than likely be the last chapter in the Tales from Korea Series. I'm thinking that maybe we should get some baby-food-sized jars, and capture the 'perfume' of Korea.

Seven million people! Can you imagine seven million people packing the streets and yelling in unison? We live some distance from downtown, and we could hear the cheering. I wonder if any structural damage was done to the downtown buildings because of the constantly yelling masses? Something to do with harmonics theory. Before 'poo-pooing' my thinking, remember the walls of Jericho. Though I suppose there was the added divine intervention.

It's been more than a month since South Korea was eliminated from the World Cup Finals, but every day they televise past games in which they were winners. I suppose it's all part of the healing process. It must have been a disappointment to have shelled out 2 billion dollars for the building of ten stadiums, and not to have won the 'Cup'. It was a very interesting experience to see so many people totally given over to a sporting event (though the political implications were overwhelming). People from all over the world were welcomed to empty their wallets and purses. Korea shed tears of joy after victories, and upon being ousted from the games in the finals, wept bitter tears of sorrow. The Koreans are a deeply emotional people. During the World Cup the Koreans were showing they could be gracious hosts. The day after Korea was eliminated from the

147

games, almost 2000 screaming Koreans staged a protest at a military installation. Now they want us to go home again. Oh well, back to business as usual.

We say *"annyeong-he-ke-sayo"* (good-bye) to Korea on Saturday. Destination - Virginia. Our military service has enabled us to live on the east coast, the west coast, many places in between, and overseas. Each move required us to alter our gardening practices and sometimes learn new gardening skills. Our motto is, 'leave the land in a better condition than when we first arrived'. I think we do that. It is difficult to leave our gardens behind. We would like to see at least one grow to maturity.

> With a pickax and shovel to boot
> We try to make the land bear fruit
> We plant grasses and trees
> Create havens for bees
> But in two or three years we uproot.

There are various reasons why Celia and I will be happy to move into our new house. One of which is we can garden without interference from others. Here, no matter what we do to try to make the yard look decent there are forces at work against us. An example, (sad but true) for two solid years we have tried to get the grass to grow on the badly eroded slope in front of our quarters (housing). The earth was parched and rocky, so we started setting aside grass clippings and leaves to add to the soil. Each time, while we were out, someone would gather the leaves and take them away. Exasperated, we decided to forgo the leaves and just sift the rocks and smooth the soil. Two days later it rained hard and the soil was washed away. After the rain we smoothed what was left of the soil (this is hard work!) and planted grass seeds. From seemingly out of nowhere, flocks of pigeons came and ate the seeds. Undaunted, we reseeded. As we did so pigeons swooped in and watched us from the roof. Much to their disappointment we covered the seeds with a black plastic mulch (Ha!). Soon we had young, succulent grass shoots nodding in the breeze and sunshine. Korean groundskeepers (men in their 60's and 70's, yup) came and cut it down to the earth (Grrrr). So we put the plastic on again and kept it on until the grass was a foot tall. Finally! Success at last (hurray). Today I returned home to find workers digging up the area so they can install a heat pump (un-believable)! I'm throwin' in the towel!!

Onward to Tales from Northern Virginia!

Glossary

Words often have more than one definition. We have listed only the meaning used in the story. You can learn more ways to use the word by checking a dictionary.

Abode—a house or home; a dwelling
Aboriginal—first people to live in a country; natives
Accommodations—lodging; rooms to live in; hotel
Accompany—to go with
Accord—will; voluntary motion
Acquaint—to make familiar; make aware
Ad infinitum—without end or limit
Ad nauseam—to the point of disgust; to a sickening extreme
Agitated—made someone anxious; moved something violently
Ahem—a small cough to fill a pause
"Ahzz"—a wordplay on the title "The Wizard of Oz", a famous movie
Akin—related; having similar qualities
Ala carté—a separate price for each item on the menu; by the bill of fare
Albeit—although; notwithstanding
Alter—change; modify; make different
Alternately—by turns; in an alternate manner
Ambassadors—representatives of one sovereign state to another state
Amenities—pleasant or desirable features
Amitabha Buddha—the "Buddha of Infinite Light", one of the five "Great Buddhas of Wisdom"
Angelic—like an angel in beauty; heavenly
Apologetic—showing realization of and regret for a fault;
Apothecary—pharmacy; drugstore
Appalled—shocked; dismayed
Apparent—clear; understood; plain
Archaic—outdated; old-fashioned
Architecture—style of building; structure; construction
Arm and leg—phrase meaning very costly; expensive in the extreme
Aroma—a pleasant odor or smell; fragrance
Array—impressive collection of something
Assassination—paid murder; killing done for money
Assemblage—a collection of people or things

Assignments—appointments of people to specific jobs and locations
Assistance—help; aid
Assumption—taking for granted; to suppose as fact without evidence
Assured—promised; guaranteed; made sure of
Astronomical—relating to the study of the universe
Attendants—people employed to serve members of the public
Auctioneer—a person licensed to sell property at a public sale
Aura—an invisible atmosphere or quality surrounding a person or place
Authentic—genuine; true
Autographs—somebody's signature, especially of a famous person
Avalanche—a sudden overwhelming quantity of something

Ballad—a romantic or sentimental song which tells a story
Ballyhoo—loud talk; noisy uproar (Colloquialism)
Banged—a series of sharp, noisy blows; slammed
Baptism—any experience or ordeal which initiates, tests, or purifies
Barbaric—primitive; lacking in civilization; unrefined
Barnyard leavings—animal manure
Beckoning—calling or summoning with a gesture
Bedecked—adorned; graced; clothed
Benefit—gain; contribute to an improvement in condition
Besieged—overwhelmed; harassed
Bewildered—confused; puzzled
Bid—command; request with authority
Big iron bird—phrase meaning airplane
Bladders—a bag in animals which holds urine
Bleary—not seeing clearly, especially due to sleepiness or tiredness
Bleat—say in a weak, trembling voice
Blemish—spot; stain; flaw; defect
Blocks—city sections or squares; the distances between streets
Bolstering—supporting with great effort
Bowled—struck down; knocked over
Brandishing—raises and moves in various directions; shakes or waves
Brine—water containing much salt; in cooking brine is used for pickling
Brink—edge; verge of something crucial
Brutish—coarse; gross; vile
Bubble wrap—plastic packaging with air bubbles for cushioning
Burbling—gurgling; bubbling sound
Butchers—those who kill animals for sale; meat seller

Cacophony—harsh, unpleasant sounds, here it is used in an unusual way to create a sense of the diverse mixture of smells
Calamity—disaster; great misfortune
Call forth—summon
Calls of nature—phrase meaning bodily need to urinate
Campaign-style—clothing with a military style or flavor in design
Canal—a man-made waterway
Cancer—a disease in which cells grow out of control
Captivating—charming, enchanting
Celebrities—famous people
Censored—deleted so as to preserve public morals
Ceremonial—an established formal ritual
Chain saws—a portable power saw with a chain possessing cutting teeth
Chalk it up—phrase meaning something is caused by something else
Champion—a valiant fighter; one who fights for another
Chaos—confusion
Chaperoned—accompanied by a person supervising behavior
Charming—delightful; giving great pleasure
Chemical—made by man using chemistry, as opposed to naturally made
Cherubic—angelic; innocent and sweet; chubby and rosy cheeked
Cherubs—angels; innocent and lovely children
Chicklets—a made-up word combining *chick* meaning baby bird and *-let* meaning little, poems and other creative writing often include unconventional or new uses of words normally understood by their context
Chocked—completely full; without room for more
Circulating—moving or passing around
Civilian—any person not in military or naval service
Clad—clothed
Claymore mines—an antipersonnel exploding device
Clutch—tight grip; hold; embrace
Coax(ing)(es)— persuades by soothing words; urging sweetly
Cobblestone—a rounded stone formerly used for paving streets
Colossal—huge; extremely large
Comfy—short for comfortable meaning cozy, snug; pleasant; agreeable
Commercials—paid advertisements
Commissary—grocery store for military personnel
Communist—supporting communism, a form of government
Compelled—driven; irresistibly urged
Complies—yields; acts in accordance with a request or demand

Complimentary—given free as a courtesy
Comprised—containing; including; consisting of
Concessions—privileges granted to someone
Concoction—a mixture of a variety of ingredients
Conditions—manner or state of being
Confrontation—hostile meeting; conflict; hostility between nations
Confucian—relating to Confucius's teachings
Conga—a dance in which dancers form a long winding line
Congestion—excessive traffic or people making movement slow
Conjunction—together; joined with; united with
Conscious—aware of; knowing
Consequently—as a result; it follows that
Construct—structure; something systematically built
Construer—translator; analyzer; interpreter
Consumed—eaten
Contain their water—phrase meaning hold the need to urinate
Contaminates—particles which make something unclean; pollutants
Contorted—twisted
Contortionists—people distorting their bodies into unnatural positions
Contracted—got; acquired
Conventional—normal; customary; ordinary; usual
Converge—come together at the same point
Conversation—talking together; a verbal exchange
Converse—talk; chat; speak
Conversion—changed from one state to another; converted; turned into
Convey—communicate; to represent
Copiously—large amounts of; plentiful; ample
Cornucopia—an overflowing fullness; plenty; abundance
Corralled—driven into (a corral)
Covertly—secretly; privately; concealed; hidden
Coveted—desirable; wished for; longed for
Coy—modest; bashful; shy
Crocks—earthenware pot or jar; vessel for holding food
Crooning—singing
Culinary—relating to cooking
Cultures—groups of people who share beliefs and practices
Curd—thickened bean paste
Curtain—to shut off or cover as with a curtain

Damage—harm; injury; adverse effect on something or someone
Deadline—time limit; the time by which something must be done
Decent—proper and fitting; satisfactory; good
Deciduous—trees which shed their leaves every year
Decorative—attractive; ornamental; looking pretty
Decrepit—broken down or worn out by long use or old age
Deem(ed)(ing)—judged; concluded upon consideration; decided
Deficiency—lacking in an essential; shortage of a nutrient
Dehydrated—dried
Déjà vu—the illusion that one has previously had a given experience
Delicacy—a choice food; a delicious, rare, or highly prized item of food
Deluge—sudden heavy downpour, a vast quantity of water
Demilitarized Zone—area from which military troops are prohibited
Demonstrations—group display of opinion; protests
Deplorable—dismal; sad; wretched; miserable
Desiccated—preserved by drying; free from moisture; dried
Desperate—in great need; extremely difficult; hopelessly bad
Diabetes—medical disorder producing excessive urine
Diameter—straight line passing through the center of a circle
Did his business—phrase meaning to urinate and defecate
Digress—ramble; move away from the topic; stray from the main subject
Din—noisy clamor; loud noise, especially of confused sounds
Dire—very bad; threatening disaster; dreadful
Disappointments—failures to attain hopes; feeling of being let down
Disarray—thrown into disorder; disorganized state; untidiness
Discerned—perceived; see or notice something; understand something
Disciples—pupil; student; learner; follower
Disclosed—reveal; make known; uncover; divulge
Discotheque—club or party with dancing
Discounted—reduced; lowered
Diseases—illnesses; sickness; ailments
Disembark—unload; land, particularly from a ship or airplane
Disembarkment— the act of disembarking or the state of being disembarked
Disintegrating—breaking into fragments
Dispenser—a device that releases its contents in measured quantities
Dispersed—scattered; caused to disappear
Disposition—one's customary frame of mind; personality; mood
Dissertations—lengthy, formal talks intended to illustrate a subject

Distinctive—unique; different; not the same
Distraction—something that interferes with concentration; diverting
Disturbing—upsetting; spoiling peace and quiet; making uneasy
Divulged—made public; revealed; told; imparted
Doozie—(also spelled doosy or doozy) slang from the 1930's meaning something outstanding
Drainage—a system of pipes to carry water away from a place
Drape—cover, usually with cloth
Dropped their loads—phrase meaning defecated
Droves—flocks; herds; large numbers
Dubiously—unsure about the outcome; feeling doubt; skeptically
Duelists—fighters in a formal armed conflict between two persons
Duplex—a two-family dwelling; a house divided into two halves
Dwindled—fell off; became less; shrunk; diminished; decreased
Dysentery—disease of the lower intestine marked by severe diarrhea, abdominal pain, and inflammation

Earthenware—containers made of baked clay
Eclectic—varied; made up of things from many sources
Economical—frugal; thrifty; efficient; not wasting energy
Edifices—buildings, especially large or impressive ones
Eerie—unnerving; spooky; inspiring unease
Egged on—phrase meaning to encourage somebody to do something, especially something wrong, foolish, or dangerous
Elation—great happiness; joy; delight; enthusiasm
Eliminated—defeated in competition
Elixir—cure-all; miraculous substance; a remedy for all ailments
Elves—in folklore, a small lively imaginary being resembling a human with long pointed ears; Santa's elves are his helpers and toymakers
Embark—begin a journey
Embarrassing—making somebody feel self-conscious or ill at ease
Embrace—adopt or take up something, especially a way of life
Enabled—made possible; provided the means to do something
Encircled—surrounded; formed a circle around; enclosed
Encompass—surround, envelop, or encircle something; enclose
Engulfed—completely absorbed; overwhelmed; swallowed up
Enlightenment—achievement of spiritual state or understanding
Entertainment—performance; exhibition; amusing show; diversion
Entrée—main course of a meal; the primary dish of food

Envision(s)(ed)—picture(s)(d); imagine(s)(d)
Episode—significant incident or event
Equipment—necessary items for a particular activity or purpose
Eroded—worn away land, usually by the force of wind or water
Escape—break free from captivity; get away; get loose; leak out
Espies—suddenly saw; caught sight of
Establishments—business premises; a place to do business
Ethics—standards of conduct; code of morality
Exasperated—greatly annoyed or irritated
Exception—something not included in the normal pattern
Excrement—waste material from the body; dung; feces
Exertions—hard effort; activity involving great physical labor
Exhaust—waste gases or steam from an engine
Existence—the presence of something in a particular place
Exodus—departure of a large number of people
Exotic—from elsewhere; unusual; unfamiliar; from a distant country
Experiences—anything observed or lived through
Extracurricular—outside of somebody's normal duties

Feat—notable act; extraordinary act or deed
Featured—distinctive part; prominently displayed item or attraction
Fertilizer hits the propeller—a cleaned up version of a slang phrase meaning when the bad things start to happen
Fertilizers—substance put on the soil to help plant growth
Fetid—having a rotten or offensive smell; stinking
Feud—a bitter prolonged dispute or quarrel lasting several generations
Finicky—fussy; difficult to please
First blast of Gabriel's trumpet—in Christian belief, the beginning of the end of the world when the faithful are called to heaven
Flamenco—Spanish dancing with hand clapping and stamping of feet
Flan—custard dessert
Flecked with foam—phrase meaning in a highly emotionally state
Flimsy—not strong; easily broken; weak
Flocks—groups of birds that travel, live, or feed together
Flotsam—debris or trash floating on water
Focal—main; principal; center
Foray—a brief journey; a short trip, usually for a particular purpose
Forecasted—predicted; estimation of what will happen in the future
Foreigners—somebody from another country; an outsider
Forewarning—warn in advance; giving previous notice to

Forgo—do without something, especially voluntarily
Forlornly—hopelessly; miserably; wretchedly
Fox and hound—pursued and pursuer; a reference to the sport of hunting foxes with packs of hound dogs as trackers
Fraught—full of problems, dangers, or difficulties
Full-fledged—fully qualifies as; completely; absolutely
Futile—in vain; having no useful effect; useless; ineffectual

Gauze—very thin, finely woven cloth
Genuine—real; having the qualities or value claimed; the phrase "genuine imitation" is often printed on goods which copy a designer's product and are, in fact, an imitation
G-force—the force of gravity, the mutually attracting force between two objects which have mass
Glazed—covered with a shiny coating
Glutinous—gluey; sticky
Gondola—a narrow flat-bottomed boat
Gorge(s)(d)—eats (ate) to excess; eats (ate) greedily
Gourmet—fine or fancy food
Graciously—kindly; mercifully; courteously
Greenhouses—glass houses used to grow tropical plants in cold climates
Gusto—zest; relish; enthusiasm; hearty enjoyment

Hacks—cough with a rasping noise
Harmonics theory—in physics, waves (for example sound, light, radio, or water) add together, if they are timed correctly and are at particular intervals in relation to one another, the power of the wave is increased. Normally, we experience this phenomenon as increased volume in sound, brighter light, a clearer radio signal, or a bigger surfing wave. The collapse of the "Galloping Gerty" bridge at Tacoma Narrows is an example of the destructive potential of harmonic waves.
Hatfields and McCoys—The Hatfield-McCoy feud (1878–1891) has become a metaphor for bitterly feuding rival parties in general. It involved two warring families of the West Virginia-Kentucky backcountry.
Haven(s)—sheltered place; a safe spot; sanctuary
Hazardous—dangerous; perilous; exposes one to injury or loss
Healing—restoring; making well; reconciling
Heck—an exclamation used instead of the swear word hell (slang); a euphemism for hell (a word used as a substitute for another in order to be less offensive is called a euphemism)

Heightened—increased; intensified; higher level of
Helicopter—an aircraft with a large propeller mounted on top of the body of the craft
Hierarchy—formally ranked group; a grading of members into different levels of status
Hilarious—extremely funny; merry; very jolly
Hindsight—understanding after the fact or event
Hitch—obstacle; *without a hitch* means smoothly, easily, or successfully
Horrendous—dreadful; very large; excessively great
Host nation nationals—The host nation is the nation which provides the location for United States forces to be stationed. Host nation nationals are citizens of the that nation, not the U.S. When U.S. military forces are stationed or live in another country, it is the result of an agreement between the host nation and the U.S. government. The agreement covers all sorts of issues including the hiring of host nation citizens (nationals) to help administer and provide the functions necessary to support the military assigned there. This includes functions like food, housing, transportation, security, supply delivery and so on.
Humanity—the human race; mankind as a group

Illegal—unauthorized; against the law; illicit; not permitted
Imitation—copied; counterfeited; faked
Impassioned—expressing strong feelings; passionate; fiery; ardent
Implications—something that is implied as a natural consequence of something else; indirect suggestion; understanding without being plainly expressed
Impolite—rude; not showing the proper manners; uncivil
Impressionable—open and easy to mold; readily impressed
Inadequate—not enough to meet the need; not equal to the purpose
Incendiary—likely to catch fire
Independence—freedom from control
Inducement—a reward to cause an action; motivate to do something
Inducted—brought in; initiated; formally included in a group
Inebriated—drunk; intoxicated
Inexorably—unstoppable; unrelenting; unchangeable
Influence—sway; to modify, change, or affect in some way
Ingested—eaten or drank; absorbed into the body; swallowed
Ingredients—component parts of a mixture, especially in cooking
Initiate—start; begin

Initiation—action which starts something; introduction to something new

Installations—places which house machinery for a particular use

Insulated—protected or isolated from something unpleasant

Intensive—concentrated; making heavy use of something

Interacts—works with

Interference—involvement in something without invitation; hindrance

Interferes—has an undesirable effect; delays the natural course of something; comes between

Interpose—place yourself between two things

Intestinal—located in the intestines; affecting the digestive tract

Inundated—overwhelmed by a huge quantity

Inverted—turned upside down; reversed

Iridescent—lustrous; having rainbow colors which appear to change as the angle at which they are seen changes

Itinerary—schedule of places to visit; plan for a journey

Jekyll and Hyde—a reference to the story by Robert Louis Stevenson titled *Dr. Jekyll and Mr. Hyde* where a doctor discovers drugs which change him back and forth between his own pleasant nature and a vicious brute; now applied to split personalities where one is good and the other evil

Jettisoned—discarded; throw something overboard

Jockeying—maneuvering or moving in order to gain advantage

Joust—medieval tournament between knights

Jousters—those who engage in combat between two mounted knights in full armor who charged at and tried to unseat each other with a lance

Jovial—merry; happy; jolly

Jungle rot—any of a number of fungal diseases which thrive in hot, humid conditions

Jurisdiction—legal power to hear and decide cases

Kaoshiung's Commeuppance—a wordplay on Montezuma's Revenge which is an offensive term for diarrhea and sickness experienced when visiting another country, originally Mexico, and eating unfamiliar food

Keen—enthusiastic; eager and willing to do something

Killer—extremely difficult

Kith and kin—somebody's friends and relatives

Laid low—ill enough to be confined to bed (Colloquialism)

Lass—young woman or girl

Lather—soapy froth; foam produced by soap or detergent with water

Latrine—a toilet for use by a large number of people; military toilet

Lava—molten rock from a volcano

Lavish—abundant; excessive; more than enough

Leaches—extracts; loses a mineral or chemical by dissolving in water

Lead—a chemical element which can poison humans and cause lower than normal levels of brain function

Leavings—scraps; left-overs; refuse; remnants

Leisurely—slow and relaxed; with no hurry; without haste

Lilliputians—small person or thing; tiny; refers to Swift's *Gulliver's Travels*, where Gulliver lands on an island inhabited by tiny people

Limbo—a state in which something or someone is neglected

Literary—related to writing

Litter(ed)—scattered over a place; things placed in disorder

Livid—very angry; furious

Loaf—quantity of bread; a portion of bread shaped and baked as a whole

Loathsome—disgusting; repulsive; odious; detestable; arousing intense dislike

Locations—place; position in space; the site of something

Locomotion—movement; power to move from one place to another

Looms—be about to happen; be imminent, often in a threatening way

Loung(ed)(ing)—lie or sit lazily; sit in a casual, relaxed way

Lower World—dwelling place of the dead; hell

Luxury—great comfort; expensive high-quality surroundings

Machetes—large heavy knives with broad blades for cutting through vegetation

Machinery—a system of mechanical parts working together

Magnum—a large bottle which holds about 1.5 liters of liquid

Mainstay—chief support; person who plays the most important role in a particular group, place, or situation

Maintaining—keeping in good repair; continuing with; preserving

Major—military rank in the Army, Air Force or Marines Corps

Manifest—appear; show

Manipulates—works; handles; treats a part of the body

Manipulation—skillful handling or operation

Marinade—a liquid or paste in which food is soaked to give extra flavor before cooking; the process of soaking the food in a flavorful mixture

Massager—someone or something which rubs or kneads the body to increase circulation and relax the muscles

Maternal—kind, caring, and protective in a motherly way

Maturity—full growth or development; mature state

Max—most; highest; maximum

Maze—puzzle of connecting paths; confusing network of streets

Medically discharged—release from military duty due to illness or injury

Meditation—pondering of something; act of thinking carefully, calmly, and seriously, especially in order to aid mental or spiritual development

Meditative—contemplative; reflective; dwelling on a particular thought

Mellows—making smoother or softer

Merengue—a ballroom dance marked by hip and shoulder movements

Miniscule—little; tiny; very small; puny

Miscommunication—unclear communication; misinterpreted exchange

Mishaps—accidents; unfortunate happenings

Missive—letter; written communication

Mom and Pop—family owned and operated; not a chain store

Mongrel—dog of mixed breed

Monsoon—rainy season; period of heavy rainfall, especially in Asia

Montezuma's Revenge—an offensive term for diarrhea and sickness experienced when visiting another country, originally Mexico, and eating unfamiliar food

Monuments—large stone statues designed as lasting tributes

Motifs—in architecture, repeated designs, shapes, or patterns

Motorized—equipped with an engine

Motto—rule to live by; a maxim adopted as a principle of behavior

Musings—thoughts; studying in silence

Mussels—edible bi-valve mollusk which live in water; in this case, the pun is from the pronunciation of the word which is similar to muscles referring to body tissue

Negotiate—cope with successfully; navigate with skill; manage to get past a hazard or obstacle

Nervously—uneasily; showing emotional tension; apprehensively

Nipping—sharp and cold; stinging cold; frosty; biting

Noticeable—easily seen; important; distinctive; noteworthy

Notorious—famous for something bad; well known

Noxious—physically harmful; poisonous; very unpleasant

No worries—Australian slang meaning do not worry; relax
Nuances—subtle differences; slight changes
Nuisance—irritating; annoying; troublesome
Numbs—with no feeling; unable to feel; takes sensation away

Obscuring—concealing from view; hiding; making hard to see
Obstacles—something in the way; hindrances; objects blocking progress
Odor—smell
Off the beaten path—phrase meaning a place not usually visited
Oily—covered with oil and, therefore, slippery
Oliver Twist—a reference to the story by Charles Dickens about an orphan by the same name who is cruelly treated and ill-fed
Opportunity—suitable time; fit time for the doing of a thing
Opt—chose from alternatives; select
Organic—relating to living things; in architecture, the forms are more flowing, twisting, and smooth rather than geometric
Orphanage—home for orphans; place for children with no parents
Ousted—forced out; removed

Paella—a dish made of saffron-flavored rice with chicken, shellfish, and a variety of other ingredients cooked together, originally from Spain
Painstakingly—showing great care and attention to detail
Paltry—insignificant; unimportant; little; slight; small
Paralyzed—caused to lose the ability to move a part of the body; unable to move
Parched—dry; lacking moisture
Par for the course—phrase meaning to be usual or expected under the circumstances
Partake—to eat or drink particularly in the company of others
Pate—head, especially the top of the head
Patrons—supporters; customers
Pavilions—outdoor structure in a park or garden used for entertainment
Pedestrians—people walking
Pediatrician—doctor for children; specialist in children's medical care
Peppered—made lively with
Perfume—pleasant scent, in this case used ironically (deliberately stating the opposite of the truth with the intention of being amusing)
Perm—same as permanent, a chemical process to curl hair
Permeates—spreads throughout; diffuses through

Perpetual—lasting forever; permanent; endless; ceaseless; constant
Persimmons—a juicy sweet smooth-skinned orange-red fruit
Perturbed—disturbed; troubled; upset; agitated
Pesticides—insect-killing compound
Photon laser—a device used for extremely fine cutting, usually in surgery
Pickled—preserved in vinegar, brine, or other liquid
Picturesque—visually attractive; pleasing to look at
Pilgrimage—journey to a holy place, made for religious reasons
Placards—plaque displayed in public with information printed on it
Plaguing—afflicting; troubling; annoying; causing distress
Plummet(s)(ed)—drop suddenly; fall straight down
Plush—rich; comfortable; luxurious (slang)
Politely—with good manners; courteously
Poo-pooing—discounting; dismissing as untrue (Slang)
Porgy and Bess—famous American opera by George and Ira Gershwin
Practice—habit; customary way of doing something
Predicament—a puzzle; a situation for which there is no clear solution, often dangerous, difficult, embarrassing, unpleasant, or, occasionally, comical
Present—give something; hand somebody something
Presents—gifts; things given to somebody to celebrate a holiday
Presume—accept as true; take for granted; suppose
Prevalent—found frequently; occurring often; widely spread
Prevented—stopped something from happening
Privacy—state of being apart from other people and not seen, heard, or disturbed by them; freedom from attention of others; seclusion
Procedure—established method; means of doing something; routine
Procession—succession; a series of things coming one after the other
Prodigy—somebody with exceptional talent at an early age
Produce—fresh fruits and vegetables
Profession—occupation requiring specialized training
Profusely—copiously; many times; expressed often
Profusion—a great deal; a large quantity of something
Progression—sequence of events; series of things; forward movement
Progressive—advanced; modern; marked by continual improvement
Promenading—leisurely walk taken for pleasure; strolling, especially in public places so as to be seen
Prominently—noticeably; conspicuously; importantly; widely known

163

Proof—evidence; something which establishes a fact; a test
Propaganda—information put out by a government to promote an idea
Protocol—code of conduct; etiquette of formal occasions; rules of correct behavior for a group
Proverbial—used to refer to a well-known phrase
Provisions—a stock of food and other supplies gathered for future needs
Proximity—closeness in space; nearness
Purported—claimed to be something

Quadrants—a quarter of an area; one-fourth of an area
Quelled—quieted; suppressed bad feeling in a reassuring way; allayed
Quest—a search for something, particularly a long or difficult one
Quirky—odd; strange

Rack—a device to torture somebody by stretching the body
Radio-controlled—remotely controlled using radio signals
Raining rhinos and elephants—a wordplay on the expression "raining cats and dogs" meaning to rain heavily; in this case the expression indicates an even greater amount of rain
Rambled—written aimlessly, not always keeping to the intended subject
Rammed—forced something into place
Rapacious—excessively greedy; ravenous; grasping
Rapscallions—naughty child; mischievous and annoying child; rascal
Raspy—say something in a harsh voice; utter in rough, grating tone
Rattling—moving rapidly; shaking something so as to cause a succession of sharp, short sounds
Ravenous—very hungry; greedy for gratification of desires
Razor wire—wire with sharp pieces of metal fixed along its length
Realization—knowing and understanding something; becoming aware
Realtor—a real-estate broker who is a member of the U.S. National Association of Realtors; a member of the association who sells property
Reassigned—transferred to another location or job; assigned again
Recitation—reading aloud or reciting from memory, especially poetry
Reconciliation—ending of conflict; renewing of friendly relationship between people or groups
Recuperate—get back; recover something which was lost
Reflection—act of reflecting something; careful thought
Reforestation—replant with trees
Regulates—controls something by rules or laws

Reigns—be the most important feature; main or most noticeable
Reindeer—large arctic deer
Relationship—connection between people; friendship
Relentless—without stopping; persistent
Remote—far away; out of the way; far from civilization
Renegade—rebel; somebody who chooses to live outside the law
Repast—meal; food
Resemble—be like somebody; similar in appearance or behavior
Resignedly—yielding; submitting; accepting something passively
Resituated—reseated; placed again
Resolutions—goals; statements of determination to complete something
Retrace—go back over, especially in the reverse direction
Reveal—make known; expose; disclose; show; expose to view
Revelations—information revealed; disclosure of something hidden
Revolving—turning; rotating; spinning; moving in a circular fashion
Ridiculously—completely unreasonable; silly; absurd; ludicrous
Robust—strong and healthy; sturdy; hale; hearty; hardy in constitution
Rocketed—moved fast; flew swiftly
Romp—run around boisterously; frolic; noisy play
Roving—moving about; traveling from one place to another
Rowdy—unruly; noisy and disorderly; rough
Royalty—royal person; king, queen, or other member of a royal family
Rugged—sharply rising or falling; rough; jagged; with irregular surface
Rumpled—untidy; disheveled appearance; with wrinkles and creases
Rumps—bottom; the buttocks
Run in—clash; row; tiff; confrontation; disagreement

Sallied forth—rushed out suddenly; any sudden start into activity
Salutation—greeting
Sarira—containing Bhuddist relics, from Sanskrit
Sauced—drunken (Slang)
Sauntering—wandering idly; walking away without concern
Scantily—inadequate; not much; meager; revealing; not covering much
Scarce—rare; being in small supply; not plentiful; few in number
Score—1. wordplay on two meanings of the word score, the first being a written version of music and the second being a colloquialism meaning a successful move, remark, or thing; 2. the number twenty
Scrumptious—first-rate; splendid; delicious
Scrunched—squeezed tightly together; crushed

165

Sculptures—three dimensional art,

Secluded—private and quiet; cut off from other places; isolated

Securing—guarding; fortifying; keeping safe; protecting

Seemingly—apparently; so far as could be observed

Seethe—be angry; violently disturbed or agitated

Self-effacement—modest and reserved; avoiding drawing attention to oneself by keeping to the background and minimizing one's own actions

Separation—state of being apart

Serenaded—sang love songs

Sewer—drain for waste; an underground pipe that carries away refuse

Shackles—restraint from freedom; hindrances; restrictions

Shady—dishonest or illegal

Shards—a sharp broken piece of glass, metal, or brittle substance

Sheepishly—embarrassed; shy; bashful

Shelled out—spent; pay out money; hand over (Slang)

Shift-like—a simple loose-fitting dress with no waistline

Shoos—says shoo and gesture a child or animal to go away

Shot—drove home; moved quickly and decisively

Sift—take something out; separate

Similitude—likeness; resemblance; condition of being similar

Sinkhole—depression in the ground; hole which drains water

Sizzle—the noise of food frying; hissing and splattering sound

Skeleton crew—minimum number of people required to do a job

Skits—short comic sketch; quick funny theatrical piece as in a revue

Slack—not tight; hanging loosely

Slooow—a deliberate misspelling of slow meant to emphasize how long something took to happen

Slurry—watery mixture

Smorgasbord—buffet; a wide selection of foods

Snarly—knotted; tangled; confused; complicated; disordered

Snatching—taking something quickly; grabbing; grasping

Snuffles—sniffs; breathes noisily through a partially blocked nose

Soothe—calm somebody down; make someone less angry or upset

Special needs—requirements some people have because of physical and mental challenges

Specialty—specialized product or service; a distinctive product

Spectacle—something remarkable to see; an impressive event

Sprint—short swift race; run quickly over a short distance

Spry—agile and energetic; brisk and active

Spuds—potatoes
Squeaks—makes a high pitched sound or cry
Squeegee—wipe away water from a surface; especially with a T-shaped tool having a crossbar of rubber or something similar
Stainless steel vats—large tubs or barrels made of metal which does not interact chemically with the contents of the vessel
Status—condition; state of being
Steeping—soaking in liquid; immersed
Stiletto—high pointed heel of a woman's shoe
Stint—allotted time; a fixed period of time spent of a task or job
Stock—standard; common; typical
Stockings—refers to Christmas stockings traditionally hung up on Christmas Eve to be filled with presents by Santa Claus
Storms—goes somewhere in an angry rush
Strait—a narrow body of water that joins two larger bodies of water
Strip-searched—literally to search a naked suspect for weapons, drugs or contraband, in this case used to indicate the detailed nature of the searches conducted on the cars entering base
Structural—relating to the construction; the way the parts work together
Stubborn—unreasonably determined; obstinate; unyielding; inflexible
Stupid—lacking intelligence or understanding; dull; slow-witted
Styrofoam—a trademark for a light plastic material used to make disposable items
Subsequent—later in time; coming after
Succulent—juicy; vital; filled with water
Succumb—give in; to be unable to resist something; yield
Suede—leather with velvety surface
Suicide bombing—a bombing attack in which the bomber intentionally dies too
Supremely—ultimately; in the highest degree; greatest
Surmise—guess about something; conclude that something is the case based on limited evidence or intuitive feeling; guesswork; conjecture
Surrendered—gave up; yielded; stopped resisting
Surrounding—encircling; enclosing; around something; associated with
Survey—look at something carefully; comprehensive study; inspect
Suspicion—mistrust; doubt; belief there is something wrong
Sweltering—very hot; sultry
Swill—to drink large amounts of something
Swooped—descended quickly and suddenly from the air

Tap—*on tap* means scheduled; planned
Tatters—ruined; torn or ragged piece of cloth; damaged state
Televise—broadcast on television
Temperatures—degree of heat; relative hotness or coldness
Terrapin—turtle; in this case, a reference to the speed of delivery indicating slowness
Thatched—roofs made of plant material e.g. straw or rushes
Thoroughbred—purebred animal, especially a horse
Thread—go carefully; move along a narrow, winding route
Tinkled—made light metallic ringing sounds; jingled
Tittering—laughing quietly; giggled in a nervous way
Toiling—working hard
Tolerance—acceptance of different views; tolerating somebody
Tome—large book
Tonic—medicine producing a sense of well-being
Torrid—1. hot and muggy; sultry 2. full of passion; ardent; zealous
Traditional—following long established customs and beliefs; customary
Tragedy—disaster; unhappy event
Trance—dazed state; in some way unaware of the environment; stunned
Tranquility—free from commotion or disturbance; composed
Translucent—allowing light to pass through
Travers(e)(ing)—go back and forth over; cross an area
Tread—walk on; step on
Trench coat—a belted double-breasted raincoat designed during World War I for the military
Trench foot—painful foot condition caused by prolonged exposure of the feet to cold and wet
Trick or Treaters—children dressed in costumes who visit neighbor's houses on Halloween and threaten to play a trick unless they are given a treat such as candy
Trundle—move slowly and heavily
Typhoons—tropical storms in the western Pacific and Indian oceans

Unaffectionately—without fondness; not lovingly
Unbeknownst—unknown; without knowledge of; unperceived by
Uncomfortable—awkward; uneasy; ill at ease
Undaunted—not deterred by the prospect of defeat, loss, or failure; not subdued; boldly continuing
Unhampered—unrestricted; progressing freely

Uniformed—wearing distinctive clothing to identify someone's job
Unobtainable—not available; can not be reached
Unsupervised—not watched to ensure correct behavior
Uproot—move somebody from a home or environment; displace
USS Cole—On October 12, 2000, the US Navy guided missile destroyer, USS Cole, was attacked in a suicide bombing which resulted in the deaths of 17 and injury to 39 sailors.
Utilizes—puts to profitable use; makes use of something

Vairocana Buddha—one of the five Buddhas of wisdom, vairocana means *Illuminator* in Sanskrit
Valiant—courageous; characterized by bravery but often ending in failure
Vantage point—position giving good view; point granting a broad view
Vast—enormous; huge in quantity; very great in number
Vermilion—bright red color
Vessels—containers for liquid
Vibrating—making small rapid movements; shaking back and forth quickly
Vigilance—watchfulness; condition of being alert, especially to danger
Vinyl—plastic compound used to make phonograph records
VIP—acronym for Very Important Person
Virgin land—land which is in a wild state; undeveloped land
Vista—scenic view; panoramic overlook
Voilá—behold; French word meaning *look there!*
Volume—amount; large quantity; mass of something

Waddle—walk with short steps while causing the body to tilt slightly from side to side, especially because of having short legs and being over-weight; gait like a duck's
Waffle—a thick pancake with a grid-like pattern on its surface
Waifs—young people with a thin fragile appearance who look needy
Warrant—serve as a reason for something; justify
Warren—crowded area with a complicated layout
Weasel—a small animal with a long body, the fur is sometimes used for clothing
Webbsicles—a wordplay on icicles, a rod of ice formed when dripping water freezes
Wheezes—breathing with hoarse whistling sound; noisy breathing

Whereby—by means of which; through which
Whimsical—fanciful; imaginative and amusing
Whines—makes a high sorrowful sound; long, plaintive cry
Whisked—moved nimbly and with speed; carried quickly
Wildebeest—gnu; large antelope native to Africa
Wilted—shriveled through lack of water or heat; drooped; weakened
Wisdom—good sense; ability to make sensible decisions; wise thinking
Won—unit of Korean currency; Korean money
Wrath—violent anger; fury; rage
Wreck—badly damaged; remains of something destroyed
Writhes—twists or squirms, especially as a result of severe pain

Zero dark...—a phrase typically used by the military to describe a ridiculously early hour for rising

Korean Phrases

As a guest in a foreign country, it is always helpful to learn to say at least a few pleasant phrases to show your goodwill and interest in the nation you are visiting. Here are a few phrases in Korean which will help you show your thoughtfulness and good intentions.

There are two major Romanization systems for transliterating Koran into English. Do not be surprised if you see the same word spelled differently. An example of the difference between the two systems is the use of the letter B or P to represent one of the Korean phonemes (individual sounds in a language). As a result Busan and Pusan are both correct spellings of the east coast port town, depending on which system is being used.

Romanization Principles used in this book.

1. Hyphens are used between the syllables of a word.
2. Spaces are used between words.
3. When the Korean letter has several Romanization options, the option which most closely resembles the pronunciation for that particular use of the letter is used.
4. An apostrophe after a letter indicates the letter is intensely aspirated (e.g. k' is *k* as in **k**ite, t' is *t* as in **t**ime, p' is *p* as in **p**uff).

Greetings:

Hello./Good morning./Good afternoon./How are you?
—*An-nyeong-ha-se-yo?*
Hello (used only when answering the phone)—*Yeo-bo-se-yo.*
Goodbye—*An-nyeong-hi ka-se-yo.* (seeing someone off)
An-nyeong-hi kye-se-yo. (leaving someone who remains)
Please.— *Put'-ak'-amnida.*
Thank you—*Kam-sa-ham-ni-da.*
Excuse me—*Shil-lye-ham-ni-da.*
I'm sorry.—*Mi-an-ham-ni-da.*
You are welcome.—*Ch'eon-man-e-yo.*
Yes—*Ye* or *Ne*
No—*A-ni-o*

171

Simple vocabulary:

And (between nouns)—*wa* (after vowels)
                          kwa (after consonants)
Here—*yeo-gi*
There—*cheo-gi*
Up—*wi-ro*
Down—*a-rae*

Simple questions:

When?—*Eon-je-yo?*
Where—*Eo-di-e-yo?*
Why?—*Wae-yo?*
Who—*Nu-gu-ye-yo?*
Which?—*Eo-neu geo-shi-e-yo?*
What?—*Mweo-ye-yo?*
How much is it? (money)—*Eol-ma-ye-yo?*
Do you speak English?—*Yeong-eo-reul hal jjul a-se-yo?*
Please give me _____. —_____ *chu-se-yo.*

Food and drink:

Coffee—*k'eo-p'i*
Ice coffee—*ais k'eo-p'i*
Juice—*chyu-seu*
Coca-cola—*k'ol-la*
Lemonade—*remon*
Cider—*sa-i-da*
Ginseng tea—*in-sam-ch'a*
Tea—*ch'a*
Milk—*u-yu*
Soup—*kuk*
Rice—*bap*
Cold noodles with beef and vegetables—*naeng-myeon*
Beef ribs—*bul-gal-bi*
Ginseng Chicken—*sam-gye-t'ang*
Fried Fish—*saeng-seon-jeon*
Stuffed Dumplings—*man-du*

Numbers:

1—*il*
2—*i*
3—*sam*
4—sa
5—*o*
6—*yuk*
7—*ch'il*
8—*p'al*
9—*ku*
10—*ship*
100—*paek*
1000—*ch'eon*
10,000—*man*
1,000,000—*paeng-man*
100.000.000—*eok*

Carry a phrase book when you travel in Korea and use it as a quick reference. Not only can you look up needed phrases, you can ask a Korean to point to the answer in your book. The literacy rate in Korea is extremely high. Almost all Koreans can read and write their own language and many can understand (although they may not feel comfortable speaking) some English.

It is worth learning to read the Korean alphabet. The alphabet is ingeniously simple and many modern Korean words have been adopted from English, so if you can sound out the word, you might just hear the English word. Examples of words which have been adopted from English include banana, piano, and computer.

To be able to better communicate, take a language class. If you are on a military post, check with the Army Community Services or similar organization for Korean classes. You can also search the internet for language classes on-line, on tape, or CD. Practice speaking Korean at every opportunity and you will soon feel more comfortable and understand more of what is being said to you.

Historical Notes:

1. Confucianism is a way of ethical thinking introduced from China emphasizing self control, adherence to a social hierarchy, and social and political order.

2. In an attempt to unify the country under communism, North Korea unleashed an attack on South Korea on June 25, 1950. The United Nations immediately called for military support of the fledgling democracy in South Korea. Sixteen nations responded including the United States. When the fight reached the Yalu River, the Chinese entered the fray and the result was a bitter, protracted conflict which devastated the entire peninsula. A complete stalemate existed by 1953 and an armistice agreement was reached between U.N. and Communist forces on July 27, 1953. The agreement established the Demilitarized Zone as a buffer between the warring factions.

3. The Japanese annexation of Korea which was officially completed in 1910 remains a sore point with Koreans. Many Korean national treasures and resources were transferred to Japan during this period. Starting in the 1930's, Korean language and culture were repressed. Koreans were treated as second class citizens and resented it. Despite their harsh treatment of the Korean people, the Japanese did much to modernize Korea. The school systems, building methods, agriculture, and industry were all impacted by changes introduced by the Japanese.

4. The spoken language of Korean is called *Hangungmal* or *hanguko*. The script in the pure Korean alphabet is called is called *Hangul* and the mixed Sino-Korean characters are referred to as *Hancha-Hangul*. *Hangul* was invented in 1443 under the reign of King Sejong in order to enable the Korean people to write their own language without the use of Chinese characters. Chinese characters were used by the upper classes, but required a great deal of education to master. *Hangul* represents words by using phonetically related letters grouped in syllables.

5. Buddhism was first adopted as a royal creed in 372 AD by the Koguryo Kingdom of the Three Kingdoms historical period. The Paekche and Shilla Kingdoms adopted Buddhism in 384 and 528 AD respectively. It remained the state religion through the Koryo Dynasty (918 to 1392 AD) and then suffered persecution through the Chosun Dynasty (1392—1905 AD) when Confucianism came to the fore. Christianity was introduced by Korean emissaries returning from China in the late 16th century.

6. Just as the English language adds foreign words to its lexicon, the Korean language has added many English words to its vocabulary. The Korean pronunciation of these words reflects the Korean letters used to spell these words and their associated sounds. Korean is a phonetic language where each letter is associated with a particular sound. In the process of adopting a word from a foreign language, the closest Korean sounds are selected and represented by the appropriate letter. This process works very well, however, because the Korean language has a different set of phonemes

(individual sounds which are used in a particular language), the resulting pronunciation sounds slightly different to the English speaker.

7. Kangwasong Fort overlooks the Kanghwa Strait. During the 1800's, Korea maintained a policy of isolation from the West. In 1866, both Russia and the United States tried to force the establishment of trade between their countries and Korea to no avail. The massacre of Catholics by the Taewon-gun galvanized the French, which were expanding their Indochina interests, into action. On October 13, 1866 the French landed troops under the command of Admiral Pierre G. Roze on the island only to be repulsed by Korean troops. Later, the U.S. State Department instructed Foreign Minister to China Frederick F. Low to negotiate with Korea for safe treatment of shipwrecked sailors. A fleet of five ships and 1,230 men sailed to Korea in May of 1871 to carry out the diplomatic task backed by a display of force. Eventually commercial treaties with Western powers were negotiated and signed in the early 1880's.

8. Seoul was the capital during the Paekchae Kingdom from 18 B.C. to 660 A.D. and during the Chosun Dynasty from 1394 to 1910 A.D. Several of the Chosun Dynasty palaces exist today, although since the palaces were built of wood, they have had to be re-built after fires. Kyongbokkung, Ch'angdokkung, Ch'anggyonggung, and Toksugung palaces can all be visited today. Kyongbokkung includes the National Museum of Korea and the National Folklore Museum on its grounds. The Olympic Park in Seoul contains

the ancient site of the Mongchon Toseong Fortress with its moat dating back to the Paekchae Kingdom.

9. Early man first inhabited Korea in the Paleolithic Age. Organized and relatively widespread governance started with the Three Kingdoms period in 57 B.C. The Three Kingdoms were Shilla (57 B.C. ~ 935 A.D.), Koguryo (37 B.C. ~ 668 A.D.), and Paekche (18 B.C. ~ 660 A.D.). The territory controlled by these dynasties was located in the deep south of the Korean Peninsula. The influence of these dynasties gradually spread northward. By 918 A.D. the remnants of the dynasties were overthrown and the peninsula was unified under the Koryo Dynasty (918 A.D. to 1392 A.D.). During this period, Korea defended itself from Mongol invasions and organized raids by Japanese pirates. The Chosun Dynasty (1392 A.D. to 1910 A.D.) swept out the Koryo Dynasty and carried out large scale land reform. The Japanese made several attempts to invade Korea during the late 1590's but were thwarted. At the outbreak of the Russo-Japanese War (1904 A.D. to 1905 A.D.), Korea declared its neutrality. Nevertheless, Japan sent troops into Korea and proclaimed military control over the whole territory of Korea. The end of World War II and the defeat of Japan, freed Korea and Republic of Korea was officially established in 1948.

Meet the authors

Mack finds inspiration for his stories everywhere and carries a notebook and pen to record them. He is a graduate of the University of Maryland and a world traveler who enjoys learning new things. His other passions include weightlifting, music, and the large organic garden he tends with his wife, Celia.

Celia loves creating beauty of all kinds. She is an award-winning photographer, a book illustrator, and multimedia artist. She also writes extensively on developing language-related skills. Celia earned a degree in Business from Indiana University, Bloomington, Indiana and in Systems Engineering from the Naval Postgraduate School, Monterey, California. A renaissance woman, she is a co-inventor of a patented antenna design. Celia served 21 years as an officer in the U.S. Army. She now enjoys gardening and creating books with her husband, Mack.

Thank you for reading this Pilinut Press book. We hope you enjoyed it!

We support our readers and educators. Our website has free lesson plans based on our books, book club support including an "Ask the Author" service, interviews with the author and illustrators, articles on developing language skills, and much more. Visit us today.

www.pilinutpress.com

Other Titles:

Can You Keep a Secret?
Danny and the Detention Demons
Little Bianca
The Snickerdoodle Mystery
Webb's Wondrous Tales Book 1
Webb's Wondrous Tales Book 2

www.ingramcontent.com/pod-product-compliance
Lightning Source LLC
LaVergne TN
LVHW011230080426
835509LV00005B/424